THE
·Basic·Basics·
COMBINATION & MICROWAVE
HANDBOOK

Carol Bowen

Grub Street • London

This revised and updated edition published 2014 by
Grub Street
4 Rainham Close
London SW11 6SS
www.grubstreet.co.uk
Email: food@grubstreet.co.uk
Twitter: @grub_street

Originally published in 1988
Reprinted 1991 (revised and updated), 1992, 1993,
1994, 1995, 1996, 1997, 1998, 2000, 2002, 2004,
2005, 2008, 2009

Copyright © 1991, 2014 Grub Street, London
Text Copyright © 1991, 2014 Carol Bowen
Design Copyright © Grub Street, London
Edited by Jenny Fleetwood

Decorative illustrations by Annie Ellis
Step-by-step illustrations by Hussein Hussein

British Library Cataloguing in Publication
Data
Bowen, Carol
    The basic basics combination
    microwave cookbook.
    1. Food: Dishes prepared using
    microwave oven – Recipes
    1. Title
    641.5 882
    ISBN 978-1-909808-07-2

Printed and bound by Berforts Group, UK

CONTENTS

THE RECIPES

MICROWAVE ROUND-UP

DEDICATION

For all microwave devotees and enthusiasts
(you know who you are).

ACKNOWLEDGEMENTS

I should like to offer my grateful thanks to the numerous microwave manufacturers who, over the years, have been kind enough to loan machines for testing, offer advice freely and generally ease the burden of microwave testing and recipe development.

FOREWORD

There can't be many cooking appliances that have had such a meteoric rise to success and ownership as the microwave cooker. Hailed as the 'un-freezer' in the 1970s when, truth be told, it did little more than defrost and reheat frozen food with a few extra basics thrown in, today it is the 'all singing and dancing' cooker valued by chefs, family cooks, singletons and all those looking for a short-cut to a nourishing meal. So much so that 9 out of 10 households in the UK now boast to owning a model.

As a long-standing microwave enthusiast I have watched with wonder at the numerous developments that have taken place over the last couple of decades as well as the amazing drop in price which has made the microwave affordable for almost all. Special developments and sales features that were just a fad have come and gone but we've retained the useful ones; refinements in design and operation have made the cooker more reliable and accurate with cooking times and results; built-in and free-standing models have found a place within the hub of the home (the kitchen) and the workplace; and power ratings have not gone over-board thereby sacrificing the quality of food cooked in the ovens at the expense of speed.

There have been some overall changes however during this time that have proved to be long-lasting and seemingly permanent. The models we had when I first wrote this book were of a general lower power rating than the average we have today. For this reason I have updated and revised this A-Z or basic, basics book of microwave cooking times and methods to reflect the current average or most popular models. This has in most cases meant a small adjustment to timings since the most common models today have a higher power rating and therefore speedier cooking time. In short, this book is more relevant to the majority of microwave cookers in homes today.

You'll still find that this is a comprehensive microwave handbook for cooking foods in a combination microwave, convection microwave or basic microwave-only cooker. So whether you want to cook a basic baked apple or poach a fish fillet, regardless of your microwave cooker type, you will find the best method and ideal timing to do so. More importantly, if there is a preferential method then it will be recommended and those foods that don't work well will be flagged up.

Of course with any new appliance it is important as a first port of call to look at your owner's handbook – this book isn't about replacing that. However, it will probably give you more detail than a handbook can possibly supply and will cover some aspects of microwave cooking that might well be assumed.

The Basic, Basics Combination and Microwave Handbook doesn't assume that you know all the basics of microwave cooking …we've included them at the front of the book for those starting out anew and they will refresh the memory of those who are more than novices. Comprehensive instructions are also given with individual entries of foods and dishes to take out the guesswork. However, if microwave cooking is still proving a little haphazard or you don't feel that you are getting the best from your machine then read the MICROWAVE ROUND-UP section at the end of the book which deals with basic management of meals and menus.

Regardless of whether you're an old-hand, beginner or some-time microwave cook, I would urge you to read the BEFORE YOU BEGIN section as a must. This has all the simple facts for following the book and getting the best from it according to your chosen model of microwave.

MAKING WAVES

Just about everyone has welcomed the microwave to the cooking scene, be they chef, professional cook, family cook, reluctant cook, snack or fast food addict. Many love the time-saving and energy-saving aspects of the microwave, others the health-promoting aspects of cooking with less fat. Whatever the reason, the general everyday tasks of cooking, defrosting and reheating foods have become easier and less troublesome with their invaluable help.

Whether you have a basic family-size standard microwave only oven or a compact, low-wattage microwave only model; a double-function convection microwave or an up-to-date multi-featured new combination oven, this book has everything you need to know to cook a whole host of basic everyday foods. However, before you start to cook, if you are a new owner or novice cook I recommend that you read the following BASIC MICROWAVE CLASS relating to your type of microwave oven. It will arm you with a whole host of basic facts, tips and procedures to follow to ensure splendid results time and time again.

BASIC MICROWAVE CLASS FOR COMBINATION MICROWAVE OVEN OWNERS

Your combination microwave oven handbook will doubtless cover the theory and principles of cooking in the combination microwave oven, and will arm you with all the specifics relating to your model. However, here is a condensed, brief explanation, or refresher course on some of the most important aspects of this method of cooking.

METHODS OF COOKING IN A COMBINATION MICROWAVE OVEN

Your combination microwave can cook in several ways: by microwave only; by convection only; by combination of microwave and convection energy; and sometimes with a grill facility. The convection energy mode may be fan or turbo assisted.

COMBINATION MICROWAVE OVEN CONTROLS

Most combination ovens allow you to select a convection temperature, microwave power level, cooking mode and time. In some cases once the cooking mode has been chosen the convection temperature and microwave level operate automatically at pre-set levels only leaving the timings to you. If your oven works like the latter then check in your handbook for details on such pre-programming for advice on which timings to follow in this book (selecting a pre-programmed setting as near as possible to duplicate the temperature and power level recommended).

PREHEATING

The question of preheating is a hot one – some manufacturers say preheating isn't necessary, others say it is for timings under a given limit, while yet others give general preheating instructions for all recipes or have a special preheating control. Always follow your individual manufacturer's advice.

COOKWARE

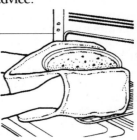

The range of cookware that can be used in the combination microwave oven is the same as for microwave only ovens with the exception of the use of metals. Some manufacturers encourage its use in all cooking modes except microwave only mode; others say don't use it at all. Again follow your specific manufacturer's advice or play safe and use a non-metallic cooking dish. One thing is for certain – you will need to use oven gloves if cooking by combination or convection only (and often with microwave only if the timings are long).

Use oven gloves when cooking by combination or convection, and with microwave if the timings are long.

EQUIPMENT

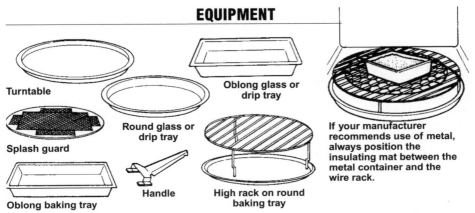

Turntable

Splash guard

Oblong baking tray

Round glass or drip tray

Handle

Oblong glass or drip tray

High rack on round baking tray

If your manufacturer recommends use of metal, always position the insulating mat between the metal container and the wire rack.

Most combination microwave ovens come equipped with a wire rack of some kind (in the larger built-in models this may just be oven wire shelving). Some models have more than one rack for specific uses (eg, grilling and baking).

Check instructions for use of the racks or position of shelving in your manufacturer's handbook. Use the wire racks at all times as they elevate the foods at the ideal height for good cooking and browning results.

Some models have a splash guard or anti-splash tray to prevent spattering of juices during cooking (especially with roasts). Use it according to instructions and make good alternative use of it as a baking tray if recommended.

If your manufacturer allows the use of metal cookware with a specially provided insulating mat then remember to position it between the metal container and the wire rack before cooking.

SELECTING THE BEST COOKING MODE

This will be a matter of personal opinion and may depend, for example, upon how much time you have, how fussy you are over browning and crisping, how the food responds to particular cooking methods; and the occasion for which you are cooking. In the instructions that follow I have given the ideal method under COMBINATION MICROWAVE but remember you can choose to cook by microwave only (simply follow the MICROWAVE ONLY instructions but remember to increase the timings by 10 seconds for every 1 minute stated – although if this is the ideal method already given under COMBINATION MICROWAVE this has already been taken into account and adjusted for you). If liked you can choose to cook by convection only too. A quick glance at the options will most surely reveal your ideal method (if in doubt generally then take a look at the chart in MICROWAVE ROUND-UP which gives an at-a-glance guide to the ideal mode to choose for certain basic foods).

COOKING BY MICROWAVE ONLY

If you are a novice microwave cook or owner and are not sure about the basics of microwave only cooking then read the BASIC MICROWAVE CLASS FOR MICROWAVE ONLY OVEN OWNERS.

CONVERTING YOUR FAVOURITE RECIPES

The best advice here is to look for a recipe or food in this book that is as similar as possible to the one you intend to cook and use those instructions and timings as a guideline. Always err on the side of safety and undercook (by under-timing). You will usually require a higher temperature than conventionally used, say 20°C higher and a low power wattage (try Low/30% power to begin with). Also follow the basic guidelines on temperatures and power levels for specific foods given in the MICROWAVE ROUND-UP section on page 135.

BASIC MICROWAVE CLASS FOR CONVECTION MICROWAVE OVEN OWNERS

Every convection microwave oven handbook covers the theory and principles of cooking in the convection microwave oven. However, here is a quick resume of the basic facts.

WHAT IS CONVECTION COOKING?

Cooking by convection is similar to conventional cooking since they both use the principle of hot air. However, in a convection oven, hot air is blown around the oven, so the whole of the oven cavity becomes the same temperature yet heats up much quicker than a

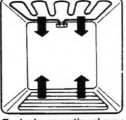

Typical conventional oven

Typical conventional fan assisted oven

conventional oven. Foods, regardless of height in the oven, will cook evenly brown and crisp and lower temperatures than usual can be used because the convection oven heats more efficiently. For the same efficiency reasons, less time is also needed to cook foods – the circulating hot air cooks foods rapidly and evenly.

TYPES OF CONVECTION MICROWAVE OVENS

Convection microwave ovens combine the two methods of convection and microwave cooking. Usually they are combined in one single oven, although some manufacturers of early models have designed two different separate ovens for this purpose.

METHODS OF COOKING IN A CONVECTION MICROWAVE OVEN

Your convection microwave can cook in several ways: by microwave only; by microwave then convection; by convection then microwave energy; or by convection only. Usually the sequence of cooking by convection then microwave can be operated automatically but the sequence of cooking by microwave then convection has to be manually operated.

PREHEATING

Most manufacturers do recommend a 10 or 15 minute preheating period for their ovens but always follow specific instructions. Ten minutes is usually sufficient for temperatures up to 200°C but 15 minutes is usually required for higher temperatures.

CONVECTION MICROWAVE OVEN CONTROLS

In most ovens you need to select a convection temperature and time; microwave power level and time; or a sequence of the convection and time then microwave and time in tandem. In the latter case the oven will usually switch from convection to microwave mode automatically. If you wish to cook by microwave then convection two separate operations and setting will be required.

CONVECTION MICROWAVE COOKING TECHNIQUES

The convection microwave will cook by microwave only (and for instructions on these techniques see the BASIC MICROWAVE CLASS on page 12) and by convection, with or without an additional microwave cooking operation. Always place foods to be cooked by convection on the turntable or convection trivet or rack supplied. Placing on the rack will ensure good circulation of hot air. If 2 level cooking is required then use the turntable and trivet and change over, if possible, halfway through the cooking time to ensure even results. If this isn't possible then remove the dish on the trivet first – it will usually have cooked faster than that on the turntable and place the dish that was originally on the turntable or base onto the trivet for the final few minutes cooking time to get evenly cooked results. Always allow a standing time of 1–2 minutes before serving.

Use the turntable and trivet if 2 level cooking is required.

COOKWARE

Manufacturers here give very specific advice and their instructions should be strictly adhered to. In general, cookware for convection cooking must be heatproof. If using the convection mode followed by the microwave mode you can generally use conventional metal baking tins, roasting tins, foil, oven to tableware, ovenable board and any trivet supplied with the oven. For microwave followed by convection cooking, it is generally advised not to use metal of any kind. Generally the no-metal rule applies for cooking by microwave only in these ovens.

EQUIPMENT

Most convection microwave ovens come with one or more baking trivets for convection cooking – these also allow 2 level baking of items such as layer cakes and biscuits. Some models also come complete with a drip pan or dish for catching juices during roasting which doubles up efficiently as a baking sheet for baked items that require some support during cooking.

SELECTING THE BEST COOKING MODE

Most manufacturers suggest using convection cooking for baking or roasting where browning and crisping are important. Buns, biscuits, scones, sponge cakes, roast joints, baked fish, pastries, bread, batters, roast vegetables and soufflé mixtures are all therefore ideal to cook by convection. Steaming, boiling and cooking that does not require browning and crisping is usually better executed through the microwave only mode. If in doubt then take a look at the chart in MICROWAVE ROUND-UP which gives an at-a-glance guide to the ideal mode to choose for certain basic foods.

COOKING BY MICROWAVE ONLY

Since this is an important and frequently used method of cooking in the convection microwave oven it is recommended that you also read the BASIC MICROWAVE CLASS FOR MICROWAVE ONLY OWNERS.

CONVERTING YOUR FAVOURITE RECIPES

When converting your own recipes generally preheat the oven, reduce the usual oven temperature by 10°C and cook for a slightly shorter length of time.

BASIC MICROWAVE CLASS FOR MICROWAVE ONLY OVEN OWNERS

There are countless cookery books on the market which explain the principles of basic microwave cooking in great detail. Your manufacturer's handbook will also have lots of information to ensure you get the best results from your own individual machine but if you want to refresh your memory on some of the more salient facts, then read on.

HOW MICROWAVE OVENS WORK

Microwave ovens simply work by converting electricity into short waves. These waves then act on the water or moisture molecules in food, agitating them to produce friction, which in turn cooks the food very quickly. Generally, because of the speed and nature of microwave cooking, foods do not brown readily.

MICROWAVE ONLY OVEN CONTROLS

Most microwave ovens today offer the cook the chance to operate the microwave oven at several different power levels. At the simplest this may be at maximum power or High (100%), Medium (50%), Low (30%) and Defrost (20%), although they may have a different description on your make of microwave. Check with the chart on page 148 and your handbook for comparison. These will enable you to cook slowly or fast rather like the temperature controls on a conventional oven and offer the cook some degree of flexibility when cooking foods of differing natures.

MICROWAVE TECHNIQUES

When we cook conventionally we employ a good many cooking techniques to ensure foods are cooked evenly. Techniques like turning over, rearranging and basting are typical ones that come to mind. Similar procedures and techniques are also used in the microwave and the following are the most frequently used.

Covering

Cover foods that benefit from keeping their moisture inside with a lid, microwave-safe cling film, greaseproof paper etc. If foods need to be kept dry and would benefit from an absorbent cover, use absorbent kitchen towel as a base for the food or a covering.

Cover fatty foods with absorbent paper to prevent splattering.

Stirring

Just as you stir in conventional cooking to distribute heat, you will need to stir during microwave only cooking. Stir from the outside of the dish to the inside.

Stir from the outside of the dish to the inside to distribute heat.

Turning over, rearranging and rotating

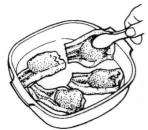

Turn foods to ensure even cooking.

Arrange food in a ring pattern and reposition once.

Rotate your food if you don't have a turntable.

When a food cannot be stirred then turn over, rotate or rearrange during cooking for even results. Most recipes will only request that this is done once, halfway through the cooking time.

Arranging foods

This is an important new aspect of cooking relevant to the microwave. Foods should be arranged so that they benefit from the wave action of microwaves in conjunction with their composition and structure. Foods that are similar in size, composition, structure and density should ideally be placed in a ring pattern

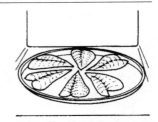

Place the thickest part of the food to the outer edge of the dish.

Arrange food around the edge in a ring pattern.

in the microwave so that they receive equal amounts of microwave energy. Irregular shapes pose a little bit more of a problem – just remember to position thicker parts to the outer edge of the dish where they receive more energy and thinner parts to the inside where they receive less.

Shielding

This conventional and microwave technique is used to protect vulnerable and sensitive areas of food. In the microwave it amounts to placing small pieces of foil on these places for part of the cooking time. It is the only time when metal can be introduced into the microwave only oven or when metal can be used during the microwave only mode of cooking in combination and convection ovens. Ensure the metal does not touch the walls of the oven or arcing can occur which could damage the magnetron.

Place small amounts of foil over food to protect sensitive areas.

Pricking to release pressure

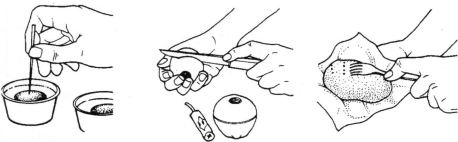

Prick the yolk of eggs, potatoes and score apples lightly to avoid food exploding or bursting.

Many foods that have a tight skin or membrane could burst during the high speed cooking times associated with the microwave – foods like jacket potatoes, baked apples, sausages etc – and these should be pricked before cooking. Less obvious might be the yolks of eggs and tight cooking pouches for foods like boil-in-the-bags.

Standing times

Foods continue to cook after microwaving due to convected heat. This residual or additional heat could overcook a food if it is not accounted for. Remember to observe standing times and to take them into account when cooking and testing foods for doneness. In many cases this may be only a few minutes but with roasts can be up to 20 minutes. In the latter case this is best done under a tent of foil, the foil placed shiny side inside over the roast.

Cover roasts with a tent of foil during standing times.

Factors and features that affect microwave cooking of foods

The density, quantity, composition and shape of food will affect how it cooks and behaves in the microwave. The denser a food is the longer it will take to cook. The more food put in the microwave the longer it will take to cook. Fatty foods and those with a higher sugar composition will generally cook faster since they attract microwave energy, and regular-shaped foods cook more evenly than irregular-shaped foods.

COOKWARE FOR MICROWAVE ONLY

Metal cookware is the real no-go area as far as equipment and cookware is concerned for the microwave only oven. This includes plates with metal trims, dishes with hidden metal bases and lead crystal. Having said that the range of cookware then is quite extensive – all the usual range of glass and ceramic ovenware, pottery, ovenproof china, roasting bags and plastic cookware can be used with the not so usual basketware, paper or boardware, greaseproof paper, microwave-safe cling film and special microwave plastic cookware.

A simple test, using a mug of water, to see if a dish is suitable for the microwave.

If in doubt then follow this simple test: Place 250 ml (8 fl oz) cold water in a glass jug in the dish to be checked. Microwave at High (100 %) for ¾–1 minute. If the water becomes hot then the dish can be used. If the dish becomes hot it is not suitable for use.

Plastics are perhaps the most difficult area to give firm and fast rules when it comes to cookware. If a plastic is dishwasher safe than generally it can be used in the microwave only oven. Melamine (often used in picnic ware) is the exception – it tends to char and distort so should never be used.

EQUIPMENT

Some microwave only models of microwave will come with a temperature probe that will allow you to cook by temperature rather than by time. Follow your own manufacturer's instructions for positioning of the probe and its use.

CONVERTING FAVOURITE RECIPES

Microwave only cooking is so specific and hard to predict that it is best to follow specially devised microwave recipes and times to begin with. When you become familiar with how your microwave performs then experiment with dishes that have some recognisable part to their make up that you can duplicate. Look in this book and other recipe books for dishes that have some familiar makeup and use their timings and instructions as a general guideline, checking constantly and erring on the short side of timings for safety.

BEFORE YOU BEGIN...

All the recipes, methods and timings in this book have been tested on 3 types of microwave oven — the combination microwave oven, the convection microwave oven and the basic microwave only oven. Since manufacturers sometimes call the convection microwave oven a combination oven the following distinction has been made.

POWER RATINGS, POWER LEVELS AND TEMPERATURE CONTROLS

Confusingly, manufacturers have developed their models of the above microwave ovens with little or no standard universal power ratings, power levels and temperature controls. For this reason I have opted to choose a set of power ratings, power levels and range of temperature controls that are used on the most popular models and they are outlined below. If your oven differs from these it does not mean that you cannot use the book, a simple adjustment may have to be made, and guidelines for these adjustments have been given.

Combination microwave oven

By this I mean an oven where a microwave cooking system can be used with a convection cooking system *simultaneously*. These ovens can also cook by microwave alone, by convection alone, or by microwave and convection modes in tandem. Simultaneous use of microwave with convection is however the important criterion. Some of these ovens also have a grill facility for use with microwave energy.

COMBINATION MICROWAVE OVENS

The most popular models have a maximum power rating of 800-850 watts (pretty much the same as convection microwave and microwave only models). Most basic models have 3–5 variable power levels and some many more. The very basic ones refer to the oven operating at the following outputs.

High (100 %)	=	800–850 watts
Medium High (70%)	=	550–600 watts
Medium (50%)	=	400–425 watts
Low (30 %)	=	250–255 watts
Defrost (20 %)	=	160–170 watts

Convection microwave oven

By this I mean an oven where the microwave cooking system can be used *in tandem* with a convection cooking system. The microwave energy can be used before the convection system or after the cooking system but never simultaneously.

The range of convection temperatures that can be used is from 140°C to 450°C. Occasionally some models of combination microwave have a narrower or wider range of temperatures to choose from. Opt for the nearest temperature and decrease or increase the times slightly accordingly.

CONVECTION MICROWAVE OVENS

The most popular models have a maximum power rating of 800-850 watts. Most have 5 variable power levels and these refer to the oven operating at the following outputs:

High (100 %)	=	800–850 watts
Medium High (70%)	=	550–600 watts
Medium (50%)	=	400–425 watts
Low (30 %)	=	250–255 watts
Defrost (20 %)	=	160–170 watts

The range of convection temperatures that can be used is from 140°C to 450°C. Occasionally some models of convection microwave have a narrower or wider range of temperatures to choose from. Opt for the nearest temperature and decrease or increase the times slightly accordingly.

Microwave only ovens

By this I mean a basic microwave oven where microwave energy is the sole cooking mode.

MICROWAVE ONLY OVENS

The most popular models for family cooking have a maximum power rating of 800-850 watts. Most have 5 variable power levels and these refer to the oven operating at the following outputs:

High (100 %)	=	800–850 watts
Medium High (70%)	=	550–600 watts
Medium (50%)	=	400–425 watts
Low (30 %)	=	250–255 watts
Defrost (20 %)	=	160–170 watts

Not all microwave ovens will have these power levels and the same description – whatever the power level guide given on your microwave all the recipes in this book can be cooked with success, providing you make the relevant adjustment (see the chart and guide on page 148 for comparative control settings).

METRICATION AND MEASUREMENTS

Both metric and imperial measurements have been given throughout the book. However, it is essential to use only one set of measures either metric or imperial since they are not interchangeable.

All spoon measures are level unless otherwise stated.

OTHER FOOD BASICS

Unless otherwise stated the following food basics apply in the recipes.
* all flour used is of the plain variety
* all sugar used is granulated
* all eggs used are medium sized
* all water used is cold (tap water temperature)
* all milk used is at chilled temperature

THE QUESTION OF CLING FILM

Government guidelines now recommend that cling film with plasticizers (ie, pvc film) should not be used as a covering or lining for foods cooked in the microwave. All cling film referred to in this book is of the special 'polyethylene' film type without plasticizers often called microwave safe cling film (and sold under such brand names as Pure Cling, Saran Wrap and Glad Wrap).

STIRRING, TURNING OVER AND REARRANGING FOODS

Specific instructions have been given for these techniques in the recipes that follow but they are based on the premise that all ovens used have a turntable or very efficient stirrer fan facility. If your oven does not have a turntable and tends to have 'hot spots' then more frequent stirring, turning over or rearranging of foods may be necessary during the cooking time.

FISH AND SHELLFISH

COD

Steamed Cod Steaks and Fillets

Arrange fish fillets in a cooking dish so that the thinner tail ends are to the centre of the dish. Fold in any flaps of skin on steaks and secure with wooden cocktail sticks. Dot with a little butter, sprinkle with seasoning and add a dash of lemon juice.

Combination microwave **Cook by microwave only.** Cover to cook and rearrange once, halfway through the cooking time. Leave to stand, covered, for 3 minutes before serving.

Quantity	Microwave Setting	Minutes
450 g (1 lb) cod fillets	High (100 %)	5–7
2 × 225 g (8 oz) steaks	High (100 %)	4
4 × 225 g (8 oz) steaks	High (100 %)	8–9½

Convection microwave and microwave only **Cook by microwave only.** Cover to cook and rearrange once, halfway through the cooking time. Leave to stand, covered, for 3 minutes before serving or using.

Quantity	Microwave Setting	Minutes
450 g (1 lb) cod fillets	High (100 %)	4–6½
2 × 225 g (8 oz) steaks	High (100 %)	4
4 × 225 g (8 oz) steaks	High (100 %)	7–8

Baked Cod Fillets

Place the fish fillets in a shallow cooking dish, dot with a little butter and season with salt, pepper and lemon juice.

Combination microwave Do not preheat the oven. Leave to stand for 2–3 minutes after cooking

Quantity	Temperature	Microwave Setting	Minutes
Per 450 g (1 lb)	250 °C	Medium (50 %)	9–14

Whole Baked Codling

Place cleaned and gutted whole fish in a shallow cooking dish and dot generously with butter.

Combination microwave Preheat the oven, if necessary, according to the manufacturer's instructions.

Quantity	Temperature	Microwave Setting	Minutes
1 × 1–1.1 kg (2¼ –2½ lb)	220°C	Low (30%)	13

Fish Cakes

Place in a shallow dish or on the combination microwave cooking rack. Brush with a little melted butter if liked.

Combination microwave Preheat the oven, if necessary, according to the manufacturer's instructions. Turn over once, halfway through the cooking time. Times refer to frozen fish cakes (chilled and fresh fish cakes will cook faster).

Quantity	Temperature	Microwave Setting	Minutes
4 × 75 g (3 oz)	250°C	Medium (50%)	5
8 × 75 g (3 oz)	250°C	Medium (50%)	7

Convection microwave and microwave only Cook by microwave only. Turn over once, halfway through the cooking time. Times refer to chilled or fresh fish cakes (thaw frozen fish cakes before cooking). If liked the fish cakes can be cooked in a preheated browning dish.

Quantity	Microwave Setting	Minutes
4 × 75 g (3 oz)	High (100%)	4

Fish Fingers

If cooking by microwave only then cook in a preheated browning dish for best results.

Combination microwave Preheat the oven, if necessary, according to the manufacturer's instructions. Turn over once, halfway through the cooking time. Times refer to frozen fish fingers.

Quantity	Temperature	Microwave Setting	Minutes
6	250°C	Medium (50%)	4
12	250°C	Medium (50%)	6½

Convection microwave and microwave only **Cook by microwave only.** Turn over once, halfway through the cooking time. Times refer to frozen fish fingers. Leave to stand for 1–2 minutes before serving.

Quantity	Microwave Setting	Minutes
2	High (100%)	1
4	High (100%)	1½
6	High (100%)	2½
8	High (100%)	3½
12	High (100%)	4

Fish Roes

Rinse the fish roes and place in a small cooking dish with a large knob of butter and seasoning to taste.

Combination microwave **Cook by microwave only.** Cover to cook and stir once, halfway through the cooking time. Leave to stand, covered, for 2 minutes before serving.

Quantity	Microwave Setting	Minutes
100 g (4 oz)	Low (30%)	4–4½
225 g (8 oz)	Low (30%)	6½–8

Convection microwave and microwave only **Cook by microwave only**. Cover to cook and stir once, halfway through the cooking time. Leave to stand, covered, for 2 minutes before serving.

Quantity	Microwave Setting	Minutes
100 g (4 oz)	Low (30%)	3½–3¾
225 g (8 oz)	Low (30%)	5–7

HADDOCK

Steamed Haddock Fillets and Steaks

Arrange fish fillets in a cooking dish so that the thinner tail ends are to the centre of the dish. Fold in any flaps of skin on steaks and secure with wooden cocktail sticks. Dot with a little butter, sprinkle with seasoning and add a dash of lemon juice.

Combination microwave Cook by microwave only. Cover to cook and rearrange once, halfway through the cooking time. Leave to stand, covered, for 3 minutes before serving.

Quantity	Microwave Setting	Minutes
450 g (1 lb) fillets	High (100%)	5–7
2 × 225 g (8 oz) steaks	High (100%)	5
4 × 225 g (8 oz) steaks	High (100%)	8–9½

Convection microwave and microwave only Cook by microwave only. Cover to cook and rearrange once, halfway through the cooking time. Leave to stand, covered, for 3 minutes before serving or using.

Quantity	Microwave Setting	Minutes
450 g (1 lb) fillets	High (100%)	5–7
2 × 225 g (8 oz) steaks	High (100%)	5
4 × 225 g (8 oz) steaks	High (100%)	7–8

Baked Haddock Fillets

Place the fish fillets in a shallow cooking dish, dot with a little butter and season with salt, pepper and lemon juice.

Combination microwave Do not preheat the oven. Leave to stand for 2–3 minutes after cooking.

Quantity	Temperature	Microwave Setting	Minutes
Per 450 g (1 lb)	250°C	Medium (50%)	9–14

HALIBUT

To Cook Halibut Steaks

Fold in any flaps of skin and secure with wooden cocktail sticks. Place in a shallow dish and dot with a little butter. Season with salt, pepper and lemon juice.

Combination microwave Do not preheat the oven. Cover to cook if liked or leave uncovered. Leave to stand for 2–3 minutes before serving.

Quantity	Temperature	Microwave Setting	Minutes
2 × 225 g (8 oz) steaks	250°C	Medium (50%)	7–11

Convection microwave and microwave only Cook by microwave only. Cover to cook. Leave to stand for 2–3 minutes before serving.

Quantity	Temperature	Microwave Setting	Minutes
2 × 225 g (8 oz) steaks	250°C	Medium (50%)	3½–4

HERRING

Fresh Whole Herring

Remove heads and clean and gut before cooking. Slash the skin in several places to prevent bursting during cooking. Place in a shallow dish and season to taste.

Combination microwave Do not preheat the oven. Cover to cook if liked. Turn over once, halfway through the cooking time. Leave to stand for 2–3 minutes before serving.

Quantity	Temperature	Microwave Setting	Minutes
Per 450 g (1 lb)	250°C	Medium (50%)	9–13

Convection microwave and microwave only Cook by microwave only. Shield the tail ends of the fish if liked. Cover with greaseproof paper to cook. Turn over once, halfway through the cooking time. Leave to stand, covered, for 2–3 minutes before serving.

Quantity	Microwave Setting	Minutes
Per 450 g (1 lb)	High (100%)	2½–3½

KIPPERS

Kipper Fillets

If buying whole fish then remove heads and tails. Place skin-side down in a shallow cooking dish.

Combination microwave Do not preheat the oven. Cover loosely if liked. Leave to stand for 2–3 minutes before serving.

Quantity	Temperature	Microwave Setting	Minutes
Per 450 g (1 lb)	250°C	Medium (50%)	9

Convection microwave and microwave only Cook by microwave only. Cover loosely to cook and rearrange once, halfway through the cooking time.

Quantity	Microwave Setting	Minutes
2 fillets	High (100%)	¾–1½
4 fillets	High (100%)	2½–3½
8 fillets	High (100%)	5–6½

LOBSTER

To Reheat Cooked Whole Lobster and Tails

Place in a shallow cooking dish and cover loosely.

Combination microwave Cook by microwave only. Turn over once, halfway through the cooking time. Leave to stand, covered, for 5 minutes before serving.

Quantity	Microwave Setting	Minutes
1 × 450 g (1 lb) whole	High (100%)	6½–8
450 g (1 lb) tails	High (100%)	5–6½

Convection microwave and microwave only Cook by microwave only. Turn over once, halfway through the cooking time. Leave to stand, covered, for 5 minutes before serving.

Quantity	Microwave Setting	Minutes
1 × 450 g (1 lb) whole	High (100%)	5–7
450 g (1 lb) tails	High (100%)	4–5

MACKEREL
Fresh Whole Mackerel

Remove heads and clean and gut before cooking. Slash the skin in several places to prevent bursting during cooking. Place in a shallow dish and season to taste with salt, pepper and lemon juice.

Combination microwave Do not preheat the oven. Cover to cook if liked. Turn over once, halfway through the cooking time. Leave to stand for 2–3 minutes before serving.

Quantity	Temperature	Microwave Setting	Minutes
Per 450 g (1 lb)	250°C	Medium (50%)	9–13

Convection microwave and microwave only Cook by microwave **only**. Shield the tail ends of the fish if liked. Cover with greaseproof paper to cook. Turn over once, halfway through the cooking time. Leave to stand, covered, for 2–3 minutes before serving.

Quantity	Microwave Setting	Minutes
Per 450 g (1 lb)	High (100%)	2½–3½

MUSSELS
Fresh Steamed Mussels

Sort the mussels and scrub thoroughly with cold running water. Place in a cooking dish with 75 ml (3 fl oz) water, fish stock or dry white wine.

Combination microwave Cook by microwave only. Cover loosely to cook and stir once, halfway through the cooking time. Remove with slotted spoon, discarding any mussels that do not open. Thicken the cooking juices with a little beurre manie if liked to serve with the mussels.

Quantity	Microwave Setting	Minutes
675 g (1½ lb)	High (100%)	5

Convection microwave and microwave only Cook by microwave only. Cover loosely to cook and stir once, halfway through the cooking time. Remove with a slotted spoon, discarding any mussels that do not open. Thicken the cooking juices with a little beurre manie if liked to serve with the mussels.

Quantity	Microwave Setting	Minutes
675 g (1½ lb)	High (100%)	4

To Bake Cooked Mussels

Remove one shell from each of the 675 g (1½ lb) cooked mussels (see above). Place in a cooking dish. Stir 120 ml (4 fl oz) cream and salt and pepper to taste into the cooking juices and spoon over the mussels.

Combination microwave Preheat the oven, if necessary, according to the manufacturer's instructions. Sprinkle with a few breadcrumbs if liked and garnish with chopped parsley to serve.

Quantity	Temperature	Microwave Setting	Minutes
1 recipe above	180°C	Medium (50%)	9

PLAICE

Steamed Plaice Fillets

Arrange fish fillets in a cooking dish so that the thinner tail ends are to the centre of the dish. Dot with a little butter, sprinkle with seasoning and add a dash of lemon juice.

Combination microwave **Cook by microwave only.** Cover to cook and rearrange once, halfway through the cooking time. Leave to stand, covered, for 3 minutes before serving.

Quantity	Microwave Setting	Minutes
450 g (1 lb)	High (100%)	4–6½

Convection microwave and microwave only **Cook by microwave only.** Cover to cook and rearrange once, halfway through the cooking time. Leave to stand, covered, for 3 minutes before serving.

Quantity	Microwave Setting	Minutes
450 g (1 lb)	High (100%)	3½–5

Baked Plaice Fillets

Place the fish fillets in a shallow cooking dish, dot with a little butter and season with salt, pepper and lemon juice.

Combination microwave Do not preheat the oven. Leave to stand for 2–3 minutes after cooking.

Quantity	Temperature	Microwave Setting	Minutes
Per 450 g (1 lb)	250°C	Medium (50%)	9

RED OR GREY MULLET
Fresh Whole Red or Grey Mullet

Clean and gut before cooking. Place in a shallow cooking dish and slash the skin in several places to prevent bursting during cooking.

Combination microwave Do not preheat the oven. Cover to cook if liked. Turn over once, halfway through the cooking time. Leave to stand for 2–3 minutes before serving.

Quantity	Temperature	Microwave Setting	Minutes
Per 450 g (1 lb)	250°C	Medium (50%)	9

Convection microwave and microwave only Cook by microwave **only.** Cover to cook and turn over once, halfway through the cooking time. Leave to stand, covered, for 5 minutes before serving.

Quantity	Microwave Setting	Minutes
2 × 250 g (9 oz)	High (100%)	3½–4
4 × 250 g (9 oz)	High (100%)	7–8

SALMON

Steamed Salmon Steaks

Place in a shallow dish so that the narrow ends are to the centre of the dish. Dot with a little butter and sprinkle with lemon juice and salt and pepper. Cover with greaseproof paper for cooking.

***Combination microwave* Cook by microwave only.** Turn over once, halfway through the cooking time. Leave to stand, covered, for 5 minutes before serving.

Quantity	Microwave Setting	Minutes
2 × 225 g (8 oz)	High (100%)	2–2½
4 × 225 g (8 oz)	High (100%)	3¾–5
4 × 175 g (6 oz)	Medium (50%)	9½–10½

***Convection microwave and microwave only* Cook by microwave only.** Turn over once, halfway through the cooking time. Leave to stand, covered, for 5 minutes before serving.

Salmon Steaks Baked in a Pastry Crust

Use 175 g (6 oz) shortcrust pastry for 2 × 200 g (7 oz) salmon steaks. Roll out the pastry thinly. Cut in half and place a salmon steak in the centre of each piece of pastry. Dot with a little flavoured butter or mayonnaise and fold up to secure like a parcel. Seal and glaze with beaten egg. Place on a cooking dish. Slash the pastry to allow any steam to escape.

Combination microwave Preheat the oven, if necessary, according to the manufacturer's instructions.

Quantity	Temperature	Microwave Setting	Minutes
1 recipe above	200°C	Medium (50%)	9–11

***Convection microwave* Cook by convection only.** Preheat the oven for 10 minutes or according to the manufacturer's instructions.

Quantity	Convection Temperature	Minutes
1 recipe above	190°C	14–19

SALMON AND SALMON TROUT

Whole Poached Salmon and Salmon Trout

Remove the head if liked. Slash or prick the skin in several places to prevent bursting during cooking. Place in a cooking dish with 150 ml (¼ pt) boiling water and a dash of lemon juice.

Combination microwave **Cook by microwave only.** Cover to cook and rearrange or rotate three times during cooking. Leave to stand, covered, for 5 minutes before serving hot or leave to cool.

Quantity	Microwave Setting	Minutes
1 × 450 g (1 lb)	High (100%)	4–5
1 × 900 g (2 lb)	High (100%)	9–11
1 × 1.5 kg (3 lb)	High (100%)	12–16
1 × 1.8 kg (4 lb)	High (100%)	17–20

Convection microwave and microwave only **Cook by microwave only.** Cover to cook and rearrange or rotate three times during cooking. Leave to stand, covered, for 5 minutes before serving hot or leave to cool.

Quantity	Microwave Setting	Minutes
1 × 450 g (1 lb)	High (100%)	3¾–4
1 × 900 g (2 lb)	High (100%)	7½–9½
1 × 1.5 kg (3 lb)	High (100%)	10–13½
1 × 1.8 kg (4 lb)	High (100%)	13½–17

SCALLOPS

Steamed Fresh Scallops

Remove fresh scallops from their shells. Place in a shallow cooking dish and cover with absorbent kitchen towel.

Combination microwave **Cook by microwave only.** Rearrange once, halfway through the cooking time. Leave to stand, covered, for 3 minutes before serving or using.

Quantity	Microwave Setting	Minutes
450 g (1 lb)	Medium (50%)	8½–13

Convection microwave and microwave only **Cook by microwave only.** Rearrange once, halfway through the cooking time. Leave to stand, covered, for 3 minutes before serving or using.

Quantity	Microwave Setting	Minutes
450 g (1 lb)	Medium (50%)	7–11

SEA BASS

Baked Whole Sea Bass

Rinse and dry the fish and season with salt, pepper and lemon juice. Place in a buttered dish and dot with a little more butter. This recipe can also be prepared using codling, grey mullet or large trout.

Combination microwave Preheat the oven, if necessary, according to the manufacturer's instructions.

Quantity	Temperature	Microwave Setting	Minutes
1 × 1 kg (2¼ lb)	220°C	Low (30%)	11–13

SHRIMPS AND PRAWNS

To Boil Raw Shrimps and Prawns

Rinse and place in a cooking dish with 600 ml (1 pt) water, a dash of vinegar or lemon juice and a bay leaf if liked.

Combination microwave **Cook by microwave only.** Cover to cook and stir once, halfway through the cooking time. Leave to stand, covered, for 3 minutes before draining to shell.

Quantity	Microwave Setting	Minutes
450 g (1 lb)	High (100%)	6½–8½
900 g (2 lb)	High (100%)	8½–10½

Convection microwave and microwave only **Cook by microwave only.** Cover to cook and stir once, halfway through the cooking time. Leave to stand, covered, for 3 minutes before draining to shell.

Quantity	Microwave Setting	Minutes
450 g (1 lb)	High (100%)	5–7
900 g (2 lb)	High (100%)	7–9

SOLE

Steamed Sole Fillets

Arrange fish fillets in a cooking dish so that the thinner tail ends are to the centre of the dish. Dot with a little butter, sprinkle with seasoning and add a dash of lemon juice.

Combination microwave **Cook by microwave only.** Cover to cook and rearrange once, halfway through the cooking time. Leave to stand, covered, for 3 minutes before serving.

Quantity	Microwave Setting	Minutes
450 g (1 lb)	High (100%)	4–6

Convection microwave and microwave only **Cook by microwave only.** Cover to cook and rearrange once, halfway through the cooking time. Leave to stand, covered, for 3 minutes before serving.

Quantity	Microwave Setting	Minutes
450 g (1 lb)	High (100%)	3½–5

Baked Sole Fillets

Place the fish fillets in a shallow cooking dish, dot with a little butter and season with salt, pepper and lemon juice.

Combination microwave Do not preheat the oven. Leave to stand for 2–3 minutes after cooking.

Quantity	Temperature	Microwave Setting	Minutes
per 450 g (1 lb)	250°C	Medium (50%)	9

SMOKED HADDOCK

Steamed Smoked Haddock Fillets

Arrange fish fillets in a cooking dish so that the thinner tail ends are to the centre of the dish. Dot with a little butter, sprinkle with seasoning and add a dash of lemon juice.

Combination microwave **Cook by microwave only.** Cover to cook and rearrange once, halfway through the cooking time. Leave to stand, covered, for 3 minutes before serving.

Quantity	Microwave Setting	Minutes
450 g (1 lb)	High (100%)	5–6½

Convection microwave and microwave only **Cook by microwave only.** Cover to cook and rearrange once, halfway through the cooking time. Leave to stand, covered, for 3 minutes before serving.

Quantity	Microwave Setting	Minutes
450 g (1 lb)	High (100%)	4–5

Baked Smoked Haddock Fillets

Place the fish fillets in a shallow cooking dish, dot with a little butter and season with salt, pepper and lemon juice.

Combination microwave Do not preheat the oven. Leave to stand for 2–3 minutes after cooking.

Quantity	Temperature	Microwave Setting	Minutes
per 450 g (1 lb)	250°C	Medium (50%)	9

Poached Smoked Haddock Fillets

Place the fillets in a shallow cooking dish with the thinner tail ends to the centre of the dish. Pour over 120 ml (8 tbsp) milk, dot with a little butter and season with salt, pepper and lemon juice.

Combination microwave **Cook by microwave only.** Cover to cook and rearrange once, halfway through the cooking time. Leave to stand, covered, for 3 minutes before serving.

Quantity	Microwave Setting	Minutes
450 g (1 lb)	High (100%)	5–6½

Convection microwave and microwave only **Cook by microwave only.** Cover to cook and rearrange once, halfway through the cooking time. Leave to stand, covered, for 3 minutes before serving.

Quantity	Microwave Setting	Minutes
450 g (1 lb)	High (100%)	4–5

TROUT
Whole Trout

Clean and gut the trout before cooking and place in a shallow dish. Slash the skin in several places to prevent bursting during cooking. Dot with a little butter if liked and season with salt, pepper and lemon juice.

Combination microwave Do not preheat the oven. Cover to cook if liked. Turn over once, halfway through the cooking time. Leave to stand for 2–3 minutes before serving.

Quantity	Temperature	Microwave Setting	Minutes
per 450 g (1 lb)	250°C	Medium (50%)	9

Convection microwave and microwave only Cook by microwave only. Cover to cook and turn over once, halfway through the cooking time. Leave to stand, covered, for 5 minutes before serving.

Quantity	Microwave Setting	Minutes
2 × 250 g (9 oz)	High (100%)	3½–4
4 × 250 g (9 oz)	High (100%)	7–8

WHITING
Steamed Whiting Fillets

Arrange fish fillets in a cooking dish so that the thinner tail ends are to the centre of the dish. Dot with a little butter, sprinkle with seasoning and add a dash of lemon juice.

Combination microwave Cook by microwave only. Cover to cook and rearrange once, halfway through the cooking time. Leave to stand, covered, for 3 minutes before serving.

Quantity	Microwave Setting	Minutes
450 g (1 lb)	High (100%)	4–6

Convection microwave and microwave only Cook by microwave only. Cover to cook and rearrange once, halfway through the cooking time. Leave to stand, covered, for 3 minutes before serving.

Quantity	Microwave Setting	Minutes
450 g (1 lb)	High (100%)	3½–5

Baked Whiting Fillets

Place the fish fillets in a shallow cooking dish, dot with a little butter and season with salt, pepper and lemon juice.

Combination microwave Do not preheat the oven. Leave to stand for 2–3 minutes after cooking.

Quantity	Temperature	Microwave Setting	Minutes
per 450 g (1 lb)	250°C	Medium (50%)	9

Poached Whiting Fillets

Place the fillets in a shallow cooking dish with the thinner tail ends to the centre of the dish. Pour over 60 ml (4 tbsp) milk or water, dot with a little butter and season with salt, pepper and lemon juice.

Combination microwave Cook by microwave only. Cover to cook and rearrange once, halfway through the cooking time. Leave to stand, covered, for 5 minutes before serving.

Quantity	Microwave Setting	Minutes
550 g (1¼ lb)	High (100%)	9½–14

Convection microwave and microwave only Cook by microwave only. Cover to cook and rearrange once, halfway through the cooking time. Leave to stand, covered, for 3 minutes before serving.

Quantity	Microwave Setting	Minutes
450 g (1 lb)	High (100%)	8–12

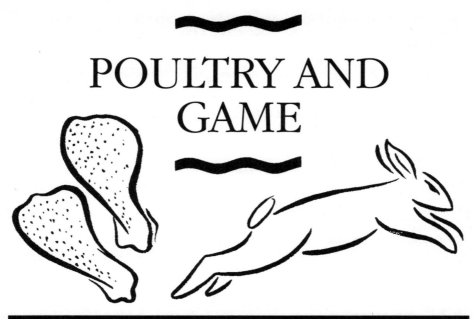

POULTRY AND GAME

CHICKEN

Roast Chicken Portions, Drumsticks, Thighs and Breasts

Prick with a fork before cooking and brush with a little melted butter if liked.

Combination microwave Preheat the oven, if necessary, according to the manufacturer's instructions. Place in a shallow dish to cook. Leave to stand for 5-10 minutes before serving.

Quantity	Temperature	Microwave Setting	Minutes
Chicken portions			
1 × 225 g (8 oz)	250°C	High (100%)	4–6½
2 × 225 g (8 oz)	250°C	High (100%)	8–10
4 × 225 g (8 oz)	250°C	High (100%)	17–21
Chicken drumsticks			
2 medium	250°C	High (100%)	2½–4
4 medium	250°C	High (100%)	7–9
8 medium	250°C	High (100%)	17–20
Chicken thighs			
8 medium	250°C	High (100%)	17–20
Chicken breasts			
2 medium	250°C	High (100%)	1½–2½
4 medium	250°C	High (100%)	3½–3¾

***Convection microwave* Cook by convection first then by microwave.**
Preheat the oven for 10 minutes or according to the manufacturer's
instructions.

Quantity	Convection/Minutes	Microwave Setting/Time
Chicken portions		
1 × 225 g (8 oz)	200°C/10 minutes	Medium High (70%)/3–5 minutes
2 × 225 g (8 oz)	200°C/10 minutes	Medium High (70%)/4–6 minutes
4 × 225 g (8 oz)	200°C/20 minutes	Medium High (70%)/7 minutes
Chicken drumsticks		
2 medium	200°C/5 minutes	Medium High (70%)/2½ minutes
4 medium	200°C/10 minutes	Medium High (70%)/3–4 minutes
8 medium	200°C/15 minutes	Medium High (70%)/5–6 minutes
Chicken thighs		
8 medium	200°C/20 minutes	Medium High (70%)/7 minutes

***Microwave only* Brush with a browning agent before cooking if liked or
crisp and brown under a preheated hot grill after cooking. Cover with buttered
greaseproof paper to cook. Leave to stand, covered, for 5-10 minutes before
serving.**

Quantity	Microwave Setting	Minutes
Chicken portions		
1 × 225 g (8 oz)	High (100%)	4–6½
2 × 225 g (8 oz)	High (100%)	9–11
4 × 225 g (8 oz)	High (100%)	17–23
Chicken drumsticks		
2 medium	High (100%)	2½–4
4 medium	High (100%)	7–8
8 medium	High (100%)	15–18
Chicken thighs		
8 medium	High (100%)	16–19
Chicken breasts		
2 medium	High (100%)	1½–2½
4 medium	High (100%)	3–3½

Whole Roast Fresh Chicken

Rinse, dry and truss the chicken into a neat shape. Season and calculate the
cooking times after weighing (and stuffing). Cook breast-side down for half of
the cooking time and breast-side up for the remaining cooking time. Cover with
foil and leave to stand for 10-15 minutes before carving to serve.

***Combination microwave* Dot with a little butter before cooking. Preheat
oven, if necessary, according to manufacturer's instructions.**

Quantity	Temperature	Microwave Setting	Minutes
1 kg (2 lb)	200°C	Low (30%)	22–27
1.5 kg (3 lb)	200°C	Low (30%)	33–40
1.8 kg (4 lb)	200°C	Low (30%)	42–55

NB. For larger birds allow 12-15 minutes at 200°C on Low (30%) power per 450 g (1 lb).

Convection microwave Preheat oven for 10 minutes or according to manufacturer's instructions. Dot with a little butter and **cook by convection first then by microwave.**

Quantity	Convection/Minutes	Microwave Setting/Time
1 kg (2 lb)	200°C/20 minutes	Medium High (70%)/7 minutes
1.5 kg (3 lb)	200°C/30 minutes	Medium High (70%)/11 minutes
1.8 kg (4 lb)	200°C/40 minutes	Medium High (70%)/15 minutes

NB. For larger birds cook at 200°C for 10 minutes per 450 g (1 lb) then for 4 minutes per 450 g (1 lb) on High (100%).

Microwave only Brush with a browning agent if liked and shield the wing tips and legs if necessary.

Quantity	Microwave Setting	Minutes
1 kg (2 lb)	High (100%)	11–15
1.5 kg (3 lb)	High (100%)	17–22
1.8 kg (4 lb)	High (100%)	22½–33

NB. For larger birds cook for 6–8 minutes per 450 g (1 lb) on High (100%).

CHICKEN LIVERS

To Cook Fresh or Thawed Frozen Chicken Livers

Rinse well and prick to prevent bursting during cooking. Place in a cooking dish with a knob of butter.

Combination microwave Cook **by microwave only**. Cover loosely and stir twice during cooking. Leave to stand for 2 minutes before serving or using.

Quantity	Microwave Setting	Minutes
225 g (8 oz)	High (100%)	2–3
450 g (1 lb)	High (100%)	5–6½

Convection microwave and microwave only Cook **by microwave only.** Cover loosely and stir twice during cooking. Leave to stand for 2 minutes before serving or using.

Quantity	Microwave Setting	Minutes
225 g (8 oz)	High (100%)	1½–2½
450 g (1 lb)	High (100%)	4–5

DUCK

Whole Roast Fresh Duck

Rinse, dry and truss the duck into a neat shape, securing any tail-end flaps of skin to the main body. Prick the skin thoroughly and place on a rack for cooking. Cook breast-side down for half of the cooking time and breast-side up for the remaining cooking time. Cover with foil and leave to stand for 10-15 minutes before serving. Crisp the skin under a preheated hot grill if liked.

Combination microwave Preheat oven if necessary according to manufacturer's instructions. Remove excess fat halfway through cooking.

Quantity	Temperature	Microwave Setting	Minutes
1.8 kg (4 lb)	220°C	Medium (50%)	29–37
2.25 kg (5 lb)	220°C	Medium (50%)	37–45
per 450 g (1 lb)	220°C	Medium (50%)	7–9

Convection microwave Preheat oven for 10 minutes or according to manufacturer's instructions. **Cook by convection first then by microwave.** Remove excess fat after convection cooking is complete.

Quantity	Convection/Minutes	Microwave Setting/Time
1.8 kg (4 lb)	200°C/40 minutes	Medium High (70%)/11 minutes
2.25 kg (5 lb)	200°C/50 minutes	Medium High (70%)/14 minutes
per 450 g (1 lb)	200°C/10 minutes	Medium High (70%)/2½ minutes

Microwave only Brush with a browning agent if liked and shield the wing tips, tail end and legs with foil if necessary. Drain away excess fat three times during cooking.

Quantity	Microwave Setting	Minutes
1.8 kg (4 lb)	High (100%)	25–29
2.25 kg (5 lb)	High (100%)	32–37
per 450 g (1 lb)	High (100%)	6½–7

GAME BIRDS

Whole Roast Game Birds

Rinse, dry and truss the birds to a neat shape. Season and calculate the cooking times after weighing (and stuffing). Bard and baste well.

Combination microwave Preheat the oven, if necessary, according to manufacturer's instructions. Turn over twice during the cooking time. Dot with a little butter before cooking and leave to stand, covered with foil, for 10 minutes before serving.

Quantity	Temperature	Microwave Setting	Minutes
per 450 g (1 lb)	200°C	Low (30%)	8–9

Convection microwave Preheat the oven for 10 minutes or according to manufacturer's instructions. Dot with a little butter and **cook by convection first then by microwave.**

Quantity	Convection/Minutes	Microwave Setting/Time
per 450 g (1 lb) minutes	200°C/10 minutes	Medium High (70%)/3½–4

Microwave only Brush with a browning agent if liked. Cover with greaseproof paper to cook and turn over twice during cooking. Leave to stand, covered, for 5 minutes before serving.

Quantity	Microwave Setting	Minutes
1 × 450 g (1 lb)	High (100%)	8–9
2 × 450 g (1 lb)	High (100%)	17–21
1 × 900 g (2 lb)	High (100%)	18½–21
4 × 450 g (1 lb)	High (100%)	32–37

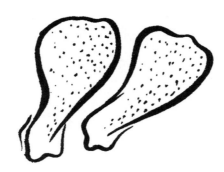

POUSSINS
Roast Baby Poussins

Rinse and dry and season well. Brush with a little butter or browning agent if cooking by microwave only.

Combination microwave Preheat the oven, if necessary, according to manufacturer's instructions. Place in a cooking dish, breast-side down and cook for half of the time. Turn breast-side up for the remaining time. An individual cooked bird may need a little crisping and browning under a preheated hot grill before serving.

Quantity	Temperature	Microwave Setting	Minutes
1 × 450 g (1 lb)	180°C	Low (30%)	14–18½
2 × 450 g (1 lb)	180°C	Low (30%)	25–32
4 × 450 g (1 lb)	200°C	Low (30%)	42–50

Convection microwave Preheat the oven for 10 minutes or according to manufacturer's instructions. **Cook by convection first then by microwave.**

Quantity	Convection/Minutes	Microwave Setting/Time
1 × 450 g (1 lb)	200°C/10 minutes	Medium High (70%)/3½–5 minutes
2 × 450 g (1 lb)	200°C/20 minutes	Medium High (70%)/5–7 minutes
4 × 450 g (1 lb)	200°C/40 minutes	Medium High (70%)/9–11 minutes

Microwave only Place on a roasting rack in a cooking dish, breast-side down. Cover with greaseproof paper and cook for half of the cooking time. Turn breast-side up, re-cover and cook for the remaining time. Leave to stand, covered, for 5 minutes before serving. Crisp and brown under a preheated hot grill if liked.

Quantity	Microwave Setting	Minutes
1 × 450 g (1 lb)	High (100%)	8–9
2 × 450 g (1 lb)	High (100%)	18½–21
4 × 450 g (1 lb)	High (100%)	32–37

TURKEY

Whole Roast Fresh Turkey

Rinse, dry and stuff the turkey if liked then truss into a neat shape. Season and calculate the cooking times after weighing (and stuffing). Divide the cooking time into quarters and cook breast-side down for the first quarter, on one side for the second quarter, on the remaining side for the third quarter and breast-side up for the final quarter. Shield any parts that start to cook faster than others with small strips of foil. When cooked, cover with foil and leave to stand for 10–25 minutes (depending upon size of bird).

Combination microwave Dot with a little butter before cooking. Preheat oven if necessary according to manufacturer's instructions.

Quantity	Temperature	Microwave Setting	Minutes
2.7 kg (6 lb)	200°C	Medium (50%)	33–38½
4 kg (9 lb)	200°C	Medium (50%)	49–58
5.5 kg (12 lb)	200°C	Medium (50%)	61–78
over 5.5 kg (12 lb), per 450 kg (1 lb)	200°C	Low (30%)	

Convection microwave Preheat oven for 10 minutes or according to manufacturer's instructions. Dot with a little butter and **cook by convection first then by microwave.**

Quantity	Convection/Minutes	Microwave Setting/Time
2.7 kg (6 lb)	200°C/48 minutes	Medium High (70%)/11 minutes
4 kg (9 lb)	200°C/72 minutes	Medium High (70%)/17 minutes
5.5 kg (12 lb)	200°C/96 minutes	Medium High (70%)/22 minutes
over 5.5 kg (12 lb), per 450 g (1 lb)	200°C/8 minutes	Medium High (70%)/1½ minutes

Microwave only Brush with melted butter or browning agent if liked.

Quantity	Microwave Setting	Minutes
2.7 kg (6lb)	High (100%)	38½
4 kg (9 lb)	High (100%)	58
5.5 kg (12 lb)	High (100%)	78
over 5.5 kg (12 lb), per 450 g (1 lb)	High (100%)	6½

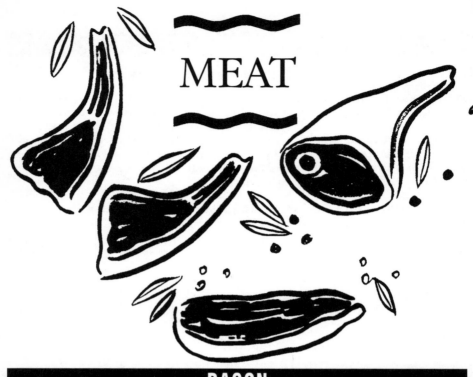

MEAT

BACON

Back and Streaky Rashers

Turn over once, halfway through the cooking time. Drain bacon on absorbent kitchen towel.

***Combination microwave* either cook by microwave only or use integral grill.** If cooking by microwave only, place on a rack and cover with absorbent kitchen towel. If grilling, place on integral high grill rack.

If microwave only

Quantity	Microwave Setting	Minutes
225 g (8 oz)	High (100%)	6½–7
450 g (1 lb)	High (100%)	13–15

If grill

Quantity	Grill Setting	Minutes
225 g (8 oz)	High	14

Convection microwave Preheat the oven for 10 minutes or according to manufacturer's instructions. Place on the trivet and **cook by convection only.**

Quantity	Convection Temperature	Minutes
225 g (8 oz)	230°C	11–14

Microwave only Place small quantities between sheets of absorbent kitchen towel on a plate, larger quantities on a roasting rack.

Quantity	Power Setting	Minutes
100 g (4 oz)	High (100%)	2½–3½
225 g (8 oz)	High (100%)	5–6½
450 g (1 lb)	High (100%)	11–13

BEEF

Roast Joint of Beef

Place the joint in a cooking dish on a rack if possible. Cover with foil after cooking and leave to stand for 10-15 minutes before carving.

Combination microwave Preheat the oven if necessary according to the manufacturer's instructions. Turn the joint over halfway through the cooking time.

Quantity		Temperature	Microwave Setting	Minutes
Per 450 g (1 lb)	Rare	220°C	Low (30%)	9
topside, sirloin	Medium	200°C	Low (30%)	12
or rolled rib	Well done	180°C	Low (30%)	15

Convection microwave Preheat the oven for 10 minutes or according to the manufacturer's instructions. **Cook by convection first then by microwave.** Turn the beef joint over halfway through the cooking time.

Quantity		Convection/Minutes	Microwave Setting/Time
per 450 g (1 lb)	Rare	180°C/10 minutes	Medium High (70%)/4 minutes
topside, sirloin	Medium	180°C/10 minutes	Medium High (70%)/5 minutes
or rolled rib	Well done	180°C/10 minutes	Medium High (70%)/6½ minutes

Microwave only Ideally place the joint on a roasting rack inside a roasting bag. Turn the joint over halfway through the cooking time. Calculate the cooking time according to weight and cook on High (100%) for the first 5 minutes then on Medium (50%) for the remaining time.

Quantity		Microwave Setting	Minutes
per 450 g (1 lb)	Rare	Medium (50%)	7–8
topside or	Medium	Medium (50%)	10–11
sirloin (boned and rolled)	Well Done	Medium (50%)	14–15
per 450 g (1 lb)	Rare	Medium (50%)	6½–7
forerib or back	Medium	Medium (50%)	12–13
rib (on the bone)	Well Done	Medium (50%)	14
per 450 g (1 lb)	Rare	Medium (50%)	10–11
forerib or back	Medium	Medium (50%)	12–13
rib (boned and rolled)	Well Done	Medium (50%)	14–15

Minced Beef

Place the beef in a dish, breaking up any large pieces.

Combination microwave **Cook by microwave only.** Cover to cook and stir twice during the cooking time. Leave to stand for 2–3 minutes before serving or using.

Quantity	Microwave Setting	Minutes
450 g (1 lb)	High (100%)	10½–13

Convection microwave and microwave only **Cook by microwave only.** Cover to cook and stir twice during the cooking time. Leave to stand for 2–3 minutes before serving or using.

Quantity	Microwave Setting	Minutes
450 g (1 lb)	High (100%)	9–11

GAMMON

Gammon Steaks

Snip the trimmed rind to prevent curling during cooking.

Combination microwave Preheat the oven, if necessary, according to the manufacturer's instructions. Place directly on the wire rack to cook, with a dish or the anti-splash trivet beneath.

Quantity	Temperature	Microwave Setting	Minutes
225 g (8 oz)	250°C	Low (30%)	5–7
450 g (1 lb)	250°C	Low (30%)	11–14
900 g (2 lb)	250°C	Low (30%)	18½–22

Convection microwave Preheat the oven for 10 minutes or according to the manufacturer's instructions. Ideally cook slices about 2 cm (¾ in) thick.

Quantity	Convection Temperature	Minutes
4 medium steaks	230°C	9–11

Microwave only Place in a dish with 150 ml (¼ pt) apple juice, cider or stock. Cover to cook. Leave to stand for 5 minutes before draining to serve. This gives a braised gammon steak – the best way of cooking gammon steaks by microwave only.

Quantity	Microwave Setting	Minutes
4 × 100 g (4 oz)	High (100%)	3½

HAMBURGERS

Hamburgers or Beefburgers

Prepare hamburgers and shape into fairly thick patties or use thawed frozen hamburgers. Ideally place on a rack to cook.

Combination microwave Preheat the oven, if necessary, according to the manufacturer's instructions. Leave to stand for 2–3 minutes before serving.

Quantity	Temperature	Microwave Setting	Minutes
per 450 g (1 lb)	200°C	Low (30%)	11–14

Convection microwave Preheat the oven for 10 minutes or according to the manufacturer's instructions. **Cook by convection only.**

Quantity	Convection Temperature	Minutes
1, 2, 3 or 4 burgers	230°C	7–9

Microwave only Ideally cook in a preheated browning dish. If this isn't possible then cook on a roasting rack and increase the times slightly. Turn over once, halfway through the cooking time. Leave to stand for 2–3 minutes before serving.

Quantity	Microwave Setting	Minutes
1 × 100 g (4 oz)	High (100%)	2–2½
2 × 100 g (4 oz)	High (100%)	3–3½
3 × 100 g (4 oz)	High (100%)	3¾–4
4 × 100 g (4 oz)	High (100%)	4–4½

KIDNEYS

Halve and core the kidneys before cooking. Dot with a little butter or brush with a little oil.

Combination microwave Preheat the oven, if necessary, according to the manufacturer's instructions. Leave to stand for 2 minutes before serving.

Quantity	Temperature	Microwave Setting	Minutes
per 450 g (1 lb)	190°C	Low (30%)	13–16

Convection microwave and microwave only Cook by microwave **only.** Ideally cook in a preheated browning dish. Turn over or stir halfway through the cooking time. Cover to cook and leave to stand, covered, for 3 minutes before serving. Time according to quality and tenderness of kidneys.

Quantity	Microwave Setting	Minutes
225 g (8 oz)	High (100%)	5–7
450 g (1 lb)	High (100%)	9–15

LAMB

Roast Joint of Lamb

Place the joint in a cooking dish on a rack if possible. Cover with foil after cooking and leave to stand for 15–20 minutes before carving.

Combination microwave Preheat the oven if necessary according to the manufacturer's instructions. Turn the joint over, halfway through the cooking time.

Quantity		Temperature	Microwave Setting	Minutes
per 450 g (1 lb)	Pink/Medium	200°C	Low (30%)	16–18
leg and shoulder joints per 450 g (1 lb)	Well Done	200°C	Low (30%)	18½–21
breast joint (boned and rolled)	Well Done	220°C	Medium (50%)	12–13

Convection microwave Preheat the oven for 10 minutes or according to the manufacturer's instructions. **Cook by convection first then by microwave.** Turn the joint over halfway through the cooking time.

Quantity		Convection/Minutes	Microwave Setting/Time
per 450 g (1 lb) leg, shoulder, fillet and breast joints	Medium to Well Done	180°C/11 minutes	Medium High (70%)/6½ minutes

Microwave only Place the joint on a roasting rack and shield any thin or vulnerable areas with a little foil. Turn the joint over, halfway through the cooking time. Calculate the cooking time according to weight and cook on **High (100%) for the first 5 minutes then on Medium (50%) for the remaining time.**

Quantity		Microwave Setting	Minutes
per 450 g (1 lb) leg joint with bone	Rare	Medium (50%)	7–9
	Medium	Medium (50%)	9–11
	Well done	Medium (50%)	11–13
per 450 g (1 lb) boned leg joints	Rare	Medium (50%)	9–11
	Medium	Medium (50%)	12–14
	Well Done	Medium (50%)	15–17
per 450 g (1 lb) shoulder joints	Rare	Medium (50%)	6½–8
	Medium	Medium (50%)	8–10
	Well Done	Medium (50%)	10–12

Chops and Steaks

Trim away any excess fat.

Combination microwave **Combination bake or combination grill as liked.** Preheat the oven, if necessary, according to the manufacturer's instructions. Leave to stand for 5 minutes before serving. If grilling place on high grill rack.

Quantity	Temperature	Microwave Setting	Minutes
4 medium chops	200°C	Low (30%)	11–13
4 lamb steaks	240°C	Medium (50%)	9–11

Combination grill

Quantity	Grill Setting	Microwave Setting	Minutes
2 medium chops	High	Medium (50%)	7–9
4 medium chops	High	Medium (50%)	9–11

Convection microwave Preheat the oven for 10 minutes or according to the manufacturer's instructions. **Cook by convection only.**

Quantity	Convection Temperature	Minutes
4 medium chops, cutlets or steaks	230°C	14–18½

Microwave only Brush with a browning agent if liked or cook in a preheated browning dish. Turn over once, halfway through the cooking time. Leave to stand for 2–3 minutes before serving.

Quantity	Microwave Setting	Minutes
2 medium loin chops	High (100%)	5–6½
4 medium loin chops	High (100%)	7–8
2 medium chump chops	High (100%)	5–7
4 medium chump chops	High (100%)	7–9

LIVER

Lamb's Liver

Trim, wash, slice and dry the liver before cooking. Place in a shallow cooking dish with a little butter and seasoning. If cooking by microwave only cook in a browning dish if liked but add the butter after preheating the dish.

Combination microwave Preheat the oven, if necessary, according to the manufacturer's instructions. Turn over and rearrange once, halfway through the cooking time. Leave to stand for 2 minutes before serving.

Quantity	Temperature	Microwave Setting	Minutes
225 g (8 oz)	250°C	Low (30%)	7–9
450 g (1 lb)	250°C	Low (30%)	13–15

Convection microwave and microwave only Cook by microwave only. Leave to stand for 2–3 minutes before serving.

Quantity	Microwave Setting	Minutes
450 g (1 lb)	High (100%)	4–5

MEATLOAF

Place your favourite 450 g (1 lb) seasoned beef mixture in a 450 g (1 lb) loaf dish, packing in firmly and levelling the surface.

Combination microwave Preheat the oven if necessary according to the manufacturer's instructions. Allow to stand for 5 minutes before serving hot or alternatively leave until cold.

Quantity	Temperature	Microwave Setting	Minutes
450 g (1 lb) loaf	200°C	Medium (50%)	15

Convection microwave Cook by convection only. Preheat the oven for 10 minutes or according to the manufacturer's instructions if necessary. Serve hot or cold.

Quantity	Convection Temperature	Minutes
450 g (1 lb) loaf	160°C	45–55

Microwave only Cook for the time below but allow a 5 minute standing time after 7 minutes of the cooking time. Leave to stand, covered with foil, for 3 minutes before serving hot or alternatively leave until cold.

Quantity	Microwave Setting	Minutes
450 g (1 lb) loaf	High (100%)	11

PÂTÉ

Pâté Maison

Line a 900 g (2 lb) loaf dish with rashers of streaky bacon. Fill with a 900 g (2 lb) seasoned puréed meat mixture (eg, 450 g [1 lb] lean belly of pork, 225 g [8 oz] lamb's liver, 225 g [8 oz] pork sausagemeat, seasoned with onion, garlic, herbs, brandy and salt and pepper) with a few strips of skinned chicken breast layered in the centre.

Combination microwave Preheat the oven if necessary according to the manufacturer's instructions. Leave to cool at room temperature then weight and chill overnight.

Quantity	Temperature	Microwave Setting	Minutes
900 g (2 lb) loaf	160°C	Low (30%)	21–22½

Convection microwave Preheat the oven for 10 minutes or according to the manufacturer's instructions. **Cook by convection first then by microwave.** Place the dish in a roasting tin half-filled with hot water. Cover the pâté with foil and cook by convection. Immediately remove the foil and set the tin aside. Cook by microwave. The pâté is cooked when the juices run clear. Leave to cool at room temperature then weight and chill overnight.

Quantity	Convection/Hours	Microwave Setting/Time
900 g (2 lb) loaf	180°C/1½ hours	Medium High (70%)/7–9 minutes

Microwave only Cover with greaseproof paper to cook. Leave to stand, covered with foil, until completely cold. Weight and chill overnight.

Quantity	Microwave Setting	Minutes
900 g (2 lb) loaf	Low (30%)	23–27

PORK

Roast Joint of Pork

Place the joint in a cooking dish on a rack if possible. Cover with foil after cooking and leave to stand for 10-20 minutes before carving.

Combination microwave Preheat the oven if necessary according to the manufacturer's instructions. Turn the joint over twice during the cooking time. Cook at the first temperature for 15 minutes of the calculated time then at the lower temperature until 5 minutes before the end of cooking. Increase the temperature again for the last 5 minutes to crisp the crackling. Alternatively cook at the optional lower temperature and power setting, turning over once, but ensuring the joint is skin side uppermost for the second half of the cooking time.

Quantity	Temperature	Microwave Setting	Minutes
per 450 g (1 lb) loin	220°C then 190°C	Medium (50%)	13–15
and leg joints	OR 200°C	Low (30%)	18½–21
per 450 g (1 lb)	240°C	Medium (50%)	9
belly of pork joint			

Convection microwave Preheat the oven for 10 minutes or according to the manufacturer's instructions. **Cook by convection first then by microwave.** Turn the pork joint over halfway through the cooking time.

Quantity	Convection/Minutes	Microwave Setting/Time
per 450 g (1 lb) loin,	200°C/10 minutes	Medium High (70%)/6½ minutes
leg and belly joints		

Microwave only Times have been given here for microwave roasting at High (100%) and Medium (50%). Both methods work well but the latter tends to give a crisper crackling to the pork joint. Turn the joint over halfway through the cooking time. Brown and crisp under a preheated hot grill if liked after cooking and before the standing time.

Quantity	Microwave Setting	Minutes
per 450 g (1 lb) loin,	High (100%)	7–8
leg and hand joints	OR Medium (50%)	11–13
on bone		
per 450 g (1 lb) loin	High (100%)	7–9
and leg joints (boned)	OR Medium (50%)	12–14

Chops

Trim the rinds of the chops and scissor snip the rind and fat if necessary.

***Combination microwave* Combination bake or combination grill as liked.** Preheat the oven, if necessary, according to the manufacturer's instructions. Leave to stand for 5-10 minutes before serving.

If microwave only

Quantity	Temperature	Microwave Setting	Minutes
4 medium loin or chump chops	220°C	Low (30%)	11–13

If grill

Quantity	Temperature	Microwave Setting	Minutes
2 medium chops	High	Medium 50%	9–11
4 medium chops	High	Medium 50%	13–16

Convection microwave Preheat the oven for 10 minutes or according to the manufacturer's instructions. **Cook by convection only.**

Quantity	Convection Temperature	Minutes
4 medium loin or chump chops	230°C	17–18½

Microwave only Brush with a browning agent if liked or cook in a preheated browning dish. Turn over once, halfway through the cooking time. Leave to stand for 5 minutes before serving.

Quantity	Microwave Setting	Minutes
4 medium loin chops	High (100%)	5–7
4 medium chump chops	High (100%)	9–10

SAUSAGES
Standard (50 g [2 oz])

Prick and place on a rack wherever possible. Turn over once, halfway through the cooking time.

Combination microwave **Combination bake or use integral grill.** If using grill then place on high grill rack to cook.

If combination bake

Quantity	Temperature	Microwave Setting	Minutes
225 g (8 oz)	250°C	Low (30%)	8–10
450 g (1 lb)	250°C	Low (30%)	9–14
900 g (2 lb)	250°C	Low (30%)	17–18½

If grill

Quantity	Grill Setting	Minutes
2, 4, 6 or 8	High	16

Convection microwave Preheat the oven for 10 minutes or according to the manufacturer's instructions. **Cook by convection only.**

Quantity	Convection Temperature	Minutes
450 g (1 lb)	230°C	14–15

Microwave only Place on a rack in a dish and brush with a browning agent if liked. Alternatively, cook in a preheated browning dish.

Quantity	Microwave Setting	Minutes
2	High (100%)	2
4	High (100%)	3½
8	High (100%)	4

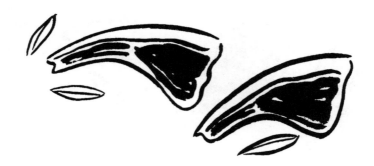

STEAKS

Fillet, Sirloin and Rump Steaks

Ideally season steaks after cooking. Brush with a little oil on both sides prior to cooking. All times refer to steaks cooked to medium/rare.

Combination microwave **Either combination bake or combination grill.** To combination bake, preheat the oven if necessary according to the manufacturer's instructions. Place steaks in a dish or on the rack. Steaks should be cut fairly thick for cooking.

If combination bake

Quantity	Temperature	Microwave Setting	Minutes
per 450 g (1 lb)	240°C	Medium	3½–4

If combination grill Preheat the grill if necessary according to the manufacturer's instructions.

Quantity	Grill Setting	Microwave Setting	Minutes
2 × 225 g (8 oz)	High	Medium	4–5
4 × 225 g (8 oz)	High	Medium	9–10

Convection microwave Preheat the oven for 10 minutes or according to the manufacturer's instructions. Place on the convection rack to cook. Steaks should be cut fairly thick for cooking.

Quantity	Convection Temperature	Minutes
1–6 steaks	230°C	10–14

Microwave only Cook with or without the use of a browning dish. If cooking without, then brush with a browning agent if liked prior to cooking. Place in a lightly oiled dish and turn over halfway through the cooking time. Cover with foil and leave to stand for 3–5 minutes before serving.

Without browning dish

Quantity	Microwave Setting	Minutes
2 × 225 g (8 oz) rump, sirloin or fillet steaks	High (100%)	4–4½
4 × 225 g (8 oz) rump, sirloin or fillet steaks	High (100%)	6¾–7½

With browning dish Preheat a large browning dish according to the manufacturer's instructions. Add a little oil and brush to coat the base. Add the steaks, pressing down well. Turn the steaks over halfway through the cooking time. Leave to stand for 1–2 minutes before serving.

Quantity	Microwave Setting	Minutes
2 × 225 g (8 oz) rump, sirloin or fillet steaks	High (100%)	1¾–2
4 × 225 g (8 oz) rump, sirloin or fillet steaks	High (100%)	3–3½

VEAL

Roast Joint of Veal

Place the joint in a cooking dish on a rack if possible. Cover with foil after cooking and leave to stand for 15–20 minutes before carving.

Combination microwave Preheat the oven if necessary according to the manufacturer's instructions. Turn the joint over halfway through the cooking time.

Quantity	Temperature	Microwave Setting	Minutes
per 450 g (1 lb)	180°C	Low (30%)	15–18½

Convection microwave Preheat the oven for 10 minutes or according to the manufacturer's instructions. **Cook by convection first then by microwave.** Turn the joint over, halfway through the cooking time.

Quantity	Convection Temperature/Minutes	Microwave Setting/Time
per 450 g (1 lb)	180°C/10 minutes	Medium High (70%)/9 minutes

Microwave only Turn the joint over once, halfway through the cooking time. Times have been given here for microwave roasting at High (100%) or Medium (50%). Both methods work well but the latter is ideal for less tender cuts or large joints.

Quantity	Microwave Setting	Minutes
per 450 g (1 lb)	High (100%)	7½–8
	OR Medium (50%)	10–11

VEGETABLES

ARTICHOKES
Globe Artichokes

Wash and dry then discard any tough outer leaves. Scissor-snip the tips from the remaining leaves and trim any stems close to the base. Place, upright, in a cooking dish and add the stock or water with a dash of lemon juice.

***Combination microwave* Cook by microwave only.** Cover for cooking and rearrange twice during the cooking time. Test if the artichokes are cooked by pulling a leaf from the base – if it comes away freely the artichoke is cooked. Leave to stand, covered, for 5 minutes before serving.

Quantity	Water/Stock	Microwave Setting	Minutes
2 medium	120 ml (4 fl oz)	High (100%)	10½–12
4 medium	150 ml (¼ pt)	High (100%)	15½–20½

***Convection microwave and microwave only* Cook by microwave only.** Cover for cooking and rearrange twice during the cooking time. Test if the artichokes are cooked by pulling a leaf from the base – if it comes away freely the artichoke is cooked. Leave to stand, covered, for 5 minutes before serving.

Quantity	Water/Stock	Microwave Setting	Minutes
2 medium	120 ml (4 fl oz)	High (100%)	9–10
4 medium	150 ml (¼ pt)	High (100%)	14–17

Jerusalem Artichokes

Peel, wash and cut into even-sized pieces. Place in a cooking dish with 4 tablespoons water or stock or 25 g (1 oz) butter.

Combination microwave **Cook by microwave only.** Cover for cooking and stir once, halfway through the cooking time. Leave to stand, covered, for 3 minutes before serving.

Quantity	Microwave Setting	Minutes
450 g (1 lb)	High (100%)	8½–10½

Convection microwave and microwave only **Cook by microwave only.** Cover for cooking and stir once, halfway through the cooking time. Leave to stand, covered, for 3 minutes before serving.

Quantity	Microwave Setting	Minutes
450 g (1 lb)	High (100%)	7–9

ASPARAGUS

Fresh Whole and Cut Spears

Prepare and place in a cooking dish. If cooking whole spears make sure the pointed heads are to the centre of the dish. Add 120 ml (4 fl oz) water.

Combination microwave **Cook by microwave only.** Cover for cooking and rearrange halfway through the cooking time. Leave to stand, covered, for 3 minutes before serving.

Quantity	Microwave Setting	Minutes
450 g (1 lb) whole	High (100%)	13–15½
450 g (1 lb) cut	High (100%)	9½–12

Convection microwave and microwave only **Cook by microwave only.** Cover for cooking and rearrange halfway through the cooking time. Leave to stand, covered, for 3 minutes before serving.

Quantity	Microwave Setting	Minutes
450 g (1 lb) whole	High (100%)	11–13
450 g (1 lb) cut	High (100%)	8–10

Frozen and Canned Whole Spears

Place frozen spears in a cooking dish with 120 ml (4 fl oz) water. Drain canned asparagus spears and place in a cooking dish.

Combination microwave **Cook by microwave only.** Cover for cooking and rearrange halfway through the cooking time. Leave to stand, covered, for 5
minutes before serving.

Quantity	Microwave Setting	Minutes
450 g (1 lb) whole	High (100%)	9½–13
425 g (15 oz) can	High (100%)	3–3¾

Convection microwave and microwave only **Cook by microwave only.** Cover for cooking and rearrange halfway through the cooking time. Leave to stand, covered, for 5 minutes before serving.

Quantity	Microwave Setting	Minutes
450 g (1 lb) whole	High (100%)	8–11
425 g (15 oz) can	High (100%)	2½–3½

BEETROOT

Fresh Beetroot

Wash but do not peel. Prick the skin with a fork and place in a dish with 60 ml (4 tbsp) water.

Combination microwave **Cook by microwave only.** Cover loosely for cooking and rearrange twice during the cooking time. Leave to stand, covered, for 5 minutes before peeling to serve or use.

Quantity	Microwave Setting	Minutes
4 medium	High (100%)	15–17½

Convection microwave and microwave only **Cook by microwave only.** Cover loosely for cooking and rearrange twice during the cooking time. Leave to stand, covered, for 5 minutes before peeling to serve or use.

Quantity	Microwave Setting	Minutes
4 medium	High (100%)	13–15

BROAD BEANS

Fresh and Frozen Shelled Broad Beans

Place the shelled fresh or frozen beans in a cooking dish with 120 ml (4 fl oz) water.

Combination microwave **Cook by microwave only.** Cover to cook and stir once, halfway through the cooking time. Leave to stand, covered, for 2–3 minutes before draining to serve.

Quantity	Microwave Setting	Minutes
450 g (1 lb) fresh	High (100%)	6½–10½
450 g (1 lb) frozen	High (100%)	10½–12

Convection microwave and microwave only **Cook by microwave only.** Cover to cook and stir once, halfway through the cooking time. Leave to stand, covered, for 2–3 minutes before draining to serve.

Quantity	Microwave Setting	Minutes
450 g (1 lb) fresh	High (100%)	5–9
450 g (1 lb) frozen	High (100%)	9–10

BROCCOLI

Fresh and Frozen Spears

Trim, wash and place in a cooking dish with the heads to the centre of the dish. Add 60 ml (4 tbsp) water.

Combination microwave **Cook by microwave only.** Cover for cooking. Leave to stand, covered, for 3 minutes before serving.

Quantity	Microwave Setting	Minutes
225 g (8 oz) fresh	High (100%)	3¾–5
450 g (1 lb) fresh	High (100%)	8½–9½
225 g (8 oz) frozen	High (100%)	7–8
450 g (1 lb) frozen	High (100%)	14–16

Convection microwave and microwave only **Cook by microwave only.** Cover for cooking. Leave to stand, covered, for 3 minutes before serving.

Quantity	Microwave Setting	Minutes
225 g (8 oz) fresh	High (100%)	3½–4
450 g (1 lb) fresh	High (100%)	7–8
225 g (8 oz) frozen	High (100%)	6–7
450 g (1 lb) frozen	High (100%)	12–13

BRUSSELS SPROUTS

Fresh and Frozen Brussels Sprouts

Trim away any damaged outer leaves and cut the base of fresh sprouts if liked. Place fresh prepared or frozen sprouts in a cooking dish with the water.

Combination microwave **Cook by microwave only.** Cover for cooking and stir once, halfway through the cooking time. Leave to stand, covered, for 3–5 minutes before serving.

Quantity	Water	Microwave Setting	Minutes
450 g (1 lb) fresh	2 tablespoons	High (100%)	6–7
450 g (1 lb) frozen	4 tablespoons	High (100%)	10½–12

Convection microwave and microwave only **Cook by microwave only.** Cover for cooking and stir once, halfway through the cooking time. Leave to stand, covered, for 3–5 minutes before serving.

Quantity	Water	Microwave Setting	Minutes
450 g (1 lb) fresh	2 tablespoons	High (100%)	5–6½
450 g (1 lb) frozen	4 tablespoons	High (100%)	9–10

CABBAGE

Fresh and Frozen Shredded Cabbage

Remove any tough outer leaves and the core of fresh cabbage then shred finely. Rinse fresh cabbage. Place fresh prepared and frozen cabbage in a cooking dish with 120 ml (4 fl oz) water.

Combination microwave **Cook by microwave only.** Cover for cooking and stir once, halfway through the cooking time. Leave to stand, covered, for 2 minutes before draining to serve.

Quantity	Microwave Setting	Minutes
450 g (1 lb) fresh	High (100%)	9½–12
450 g (1 lb) frozen	High (100%)	8½–10½

Convection microwave and microwave only **Cook by microwave only.** Cover for cooking and stir once, halfway through the cooking time. Leave to stand, covered, for 2 minutes before draining to serve.

Quantity	Microwave Setting	Minutes
450 g (1 lb) fresh	High (100%)	8–10
450 g (1 lb) frozen	High (100%)	7–9

CARROTS

Fresh and Frozen Whole and Sliced

Peel or scrub fresh carrots and slice if liked. Place fresh or frozen whole or sliced carrots in a cooking dish. Add 60 ml (4 tbsp) water to fresh carrots and 30 ml (2 tbsp) water to frozen carrots.

Combination microwave **Cook by microwave only.** Cover for cooking and stir once, halfway through the cooking time. Leave to stand, covered, for 2-5 minutes before serving.

Quantity	Microwave Setting	Minutes
450 g (1 lb) fresh whole	High (100%)	13–15½
450 g (1 lb) fresh sliced	High (100%)	10½–13
450 g (1 lb) frozen whole	High (100%)	10½–13
450 g (1 lb) frozen sliced	High (100%)	8½–10½

Convection microwave and microwave only **Cook by microwave only.** Cover for cooking and stir once, halfway through the cooking time. Leave to stand, covered, for 2-5 minutes before serving.

Quantity	Microwave Setting	Minutes
450 g (1 lb) fresh whole	High (100%)	11–13
450 g (1 lb) fresh sliced	High (100%)	9–11
450 g (1 lb) frozen whole	High (100%)	9–11
450 g (1 lb) frozen sliced	High (100%)	7–9

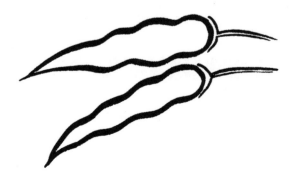

CAULIFLOWER

Fresh and Frozen Cauliflower Florets

Trim fresh cauliflower into even-sized florets. Place fresh and frozen florets in a cooking dish and add 60 ml (4 tbsp) water.

Combination microwave **Cook by microwave only.** Cover for cooking and stir once, halfway through the cooking time. Leave to stand, covered, for 3–5 minutes before serving.

Quantity	Microwave Setting	Minutes
450 g (1 lb) fresh	High (100%)	11–13
450 g (1 lb) frozen	High (100%)	8½–9½

Convection microwave and microwave only Cook by microwave only. Cover for cooking and stir once, halfway through the cooking time. Leave to stand, covered, for 3–5 minutes before serving.

Quantity	Microwave Setting	Minutes
450 g (1 lb) fresh	High (100%)	9–11
450 g (1 lb) frozen	High (100%)	7–8

CELERY

Fresh Sliced Celery and Celery Hearts

Scrub and slice celery sticks or wash and halve celery hearts, lengthways. Place slices or hearts in a cooking dish with 30 ml (2 tbsp) water and a knob of butter (optional).

Combination microwave **Cook by microwave only.** Cover for cooking and stir or rearrange and turn over once, halfway through the cooking time. Leave to stand, covered, for 3 minutes before serving.

Quantity	Microwave Setting	Minutes
1 medium head, sliced	High (100%)	5–6
4 hearts	High (100%)	4–5

Convection microwave and microwave only **Cook by microwave only.** Cover for cooking and stir or rearrange and turn over once, halfway through the cooking time. Leave to stand, covered, for 3 minutes before serving.

Quantity	Microwave Setting	Minutes
1 medium head, sliced	High (100%)	4–5
4 hearts	High (100%)	3¾–4

CORN ON THE COB

Fresh Husked Corn on the Cob

Remove the husks and any silky threads and wash well. Wrap individually in microwave cling film or place in a cooking dish with 60 ml (4 tbsp) water.

***Combination microwave* Cook by microwave only.** Cover if cooking in a dish and turn over and rearrange once, halfway through the cooking time. Leave to stand, covered, for 3–5 minutes before serving.

Quantity	Microwave Setting	Minutes
1 medium cob	High (100%)	3–3¾
2 medium cobs	High (100%)	5–6
3 medium cobs	High (100%)	7–8½
4 medium cobs	High (100%)	9½–10½

***Convection microwave and microwave only* Cook by microwave only.** Cover if cooking in a dish and turn over and rearrange once, halfway through the cooking time. Leave to stand, covered, for 3–5 minutes before serving.

Quantity	Microwave Setting	Minutes
1 medium cob	High (100%)	2½–3½
2 medium cobs	High (100%)	4–5
3 medium cobs	High (100%)	6–7
4 medium cobs	High (100%)	8–9

COURGETTES

Fresh and Frozen Sliced Courgettes

Trim the ends and thinly slice fresh courgettes. Place fresh or frozen sliced courgettes in a cooking dish with a knob of butter.

Combination microwave **Cook by microwave only.** Cover loosely for cooking and stir once, halfway through the cooking time. Leave to stand, covered, for 2–3 minutes before serving.

Quantity	Microwave Setting	Minutes
450 g (1 lb) fresh	High (100%)	6–8
450 g (1 lb) frozen	High (100%)	7–8½

Convection microwave and microwave only **Cook by microwave only.** Cover loosely for cooking and stir once, halfway through the cooking time. Leave to stand, covered, for 2–3 minutes before serving.

Quantity	Microwave Setting	Minutes
450 g (1 lb) fresh	High (100%)	5–7
450 g (1 lb) frozen	High (100%)	6–7

FENNEL

Fresh Sliced Fennel

Trim and slice thinly. Place in a cooking dish with 45 ml (3 tbsp) water.

Combination microwave **Cook by microwave only.** Cover to cook and stir once, halfway through the cooking time. Leave to stand, covered, for 2–3 minutes before serving or using.

Quantity	Microwave Setting	Minutes
450 g (1 lb)	High (100%)	9½–10½

Convection microwave and microwave only **Cook by microwave only.** Cover to cook and stir once, halfway through the cooking time. Leave to stand, covered, for 2–3 minutes before serving or using.

Quantity	Microwave Setting	Minutes
450 g (1 lb)	High (100%)	8–9

63

GREEN BEANS

Fresh and Frozen Whole, Cut and Sliced Green Beans

Place prepared or frozen beans in a cooking dish with 60 ml (4 tbsp) water.

***Combination microwave* Cook by microwave only.** Cover for cooking and stir once, halfway through the cooking time.

Quantity	Microwave Setting	Minutes
450 g (1 lb) fresh whole green beans	High (100%)	16½-20½
450 g (1 lb) fresh cut green beans	High (100%)	13–16½
450 g (1 lb) fresh whole French beans	High (100%)	13–16½
450 g (1 lb) fresh sliced runner beans	High (100%)	13–16½
450 g (1 lb) frozen whole green beans	High (100%)	15-16½
450 g (1 lb) frozen cut green beans	High (100%)	10½–13
450 g (1 lb) frozen whole French beans	High (100%)	14–16½
450 g (1 lb) frozen sliced runner beans	High (100%)	10½–13

***Convection microwave and microwave only* Cook by microwave only.** Cover for cooking and stir once, halfway through the cooking time.

Quantity	Microwave Setting	Minutes
450 g (1 lb) fresh whole green beans	High (100%)	14–17
450 g (1 lb) fresh cut green beans	High (100%)	11–14
450 g (1 lb) fresh whole French beans	High (100%)	11–14
450 g (1 lb) fresh sliced runner beans	High (100%)	11–14
450 g (1 lb) frozen whole green beans	High (100%)	13–14
450 g (1 lb) frozen cut green beans	High (100%)	9–11
450 g (1 lb) frozen whole French beans	High (100%)	12–14
450 g (1 lb) frozen sliced runner beans	High (100%)	9–11

KALE

Fresh Curly Kale

Trim away the thick stalks and stems and shred. Rinse and place in a cooking dish with 150 ml (¼ pt) water.

***Combination microwave* Cook by microwave only.** Cover for cooking and stir every 5 minutes of the cooking time. Leave to stand for 2 minutes before draining to serve.

Quantity	Microwave Setting	Minutes
450 g (1 lb)	High (100%)	16½–18½

Convection microwave and microwave only **Cook** by microwave **only.** Cover for cooking and stir every 5 minutes of the cooking time. Leave to stand for 2 minutes before draining to serve.

Quantity	Microwave Setting	Minutes
450 g (1 lb)	High (100%)	14–16

LEEKS

Fresh and Frozen Whole and Sliced Leeks

Trim whole leeks and make a few deep slits into each leek from top to bottom. Thinly slice whole leeks. Place whole, sliced fresh or frozen sliced in a cooking dish with 75 ml (5 tbsp) water.

Combination microwave **Cook by microwave only.** Cover for cooking and stir or rearrange once, halfway through the cooking time. Leave to stand, covered, for 3–5 minutes before draining to serve or use.

Quantity	Microwave Setting	Minutes
450 g (1 lb) fresh whole	High (100%)	3–5
450 g (1 lb) fresh sliced	High (100%)	8–10½
450 g (1 lb) frozen sliced	High (100%)	12–13

Convection microwave and microwave only **Cook** by microwave **only.** Cover for cooking and stir or rearrange once, halfway through the cooking time. Leave to stand, covered, for 3–5 minutes before draining to serve or use.

Quantity	Microwave Setting	Minutes
450 g (1 lb) fresh whole	High (100%)	2½–4
450 g (1 lb) fresh sliced	High (100%)	7–9
450 g (1 lb) frozen sliced	High (100%)	10–11

MANGETOUT

Fresh and Frozen Mangetout

Trim fresh mangetout but leave whole. Place fresh or frozen whole mangetout in a cooking dish with 30 ml (2 tbsp) water.

Combination microwave **Cook by microwave only.** Cover for cooking and stir once, halfway through the cooking time. Leave to stand, covered, for 2 minutes before serving.

Quantity	Microwave Setting	Minutes
225 g (8 oz) fresh	High (100%)	3¾–5
225 g (8 oz) frozen	High (100%)	3–3¾

Convection microwave and microwave only **Cook by microwave only.** Cover for cooking and stir once, halfway through the cooking time. Leave to stand, covered, for 2 minutes before serving.

Quantity	Microwave Setting	Minutes
225 g (8 oz) fresh	High (100%)	3½–4
225 g (8 oz) frozen	High (100%)	2½–3½

MARROW

Fresh Cubed

Peel, seed and dice fresh marrow. Place in a cooking dish without any extra water.

Combination microwave **Cook by microwave only.** Cover for cooking and stir once, halfway through the cooking time. Leave to stand, covered, for 2–3 minutes before serving.

Quantity	Microwave Setting	Minutes
450 g (1 lb)	High (100%)	7–10½

Convection microwave and microwave only **Cook by microwave only.** Cover for cooking and stir once, halfway through the cooking time. Leave to stand, covered, for 2–3 minutes before serving.

Quantity	Microwave Setting	Minutes
450 g (1 lb)	High (100%)	6–9

MIXED VEGETABLES
Frozen Diced Mixed Vegetables

Place in a cooking dish with 30 ml (2 tbsp) water.

Combination microwave **Cook by microwave only.** Cover to cook and stir once, halfway through the cooking time. Leave to stand, covered, for 2 minutes before serving.

Quantity	Microwave Setting	Minutes
225 g (8 oz)	High (100%)	3½–4
450 g (1 lb)	High (100%)	6½–7

Convection microwave and microwave only **Cook by microwave only.** Cover to cook and stir once, halfway through the cooking time. Leave to stand, covered, for 2 minutes before serving.

Quantity	Microwave Setting	Minutes
225 g (8 oz)	High (100%)	3½–4
450 g (1 lb)	High (100%)	6½–7

MUSHROOMS
Fresh Whole and Sliced

Wipe and trim and slice if liked. Place in a cooking dish with a knob of butter and 30 ml (2 tbsp) water.

Combination microwave **Cook by microwave only.** Cover to cook and stir once, halfway through the cooking time. Leave to stand, covered, for 1–2 minutes before serving.

Quantity	Microwave Setting	Minutes
450 g (8 oz) whole	High (100%)	3¾–5
450 g (1 lb) sliced	High (100%)	3–3¾

Convection microwave and microwave only **Cook by microwave only.** Cover to cook and stir once, halfway through the cooking time. Leave to stand, covered, for 1–2 minutes before serving.

Quantity	Microwave Setting	Minutes
450 g (1 lb) whole	High (100%)	3½–4
450 g (1 lb) sliced	High (100%)	2½–3½

Frozen and Canned Mushrooms

Place frozen mushrooms in a cooking dish with a knob of butter. Place canned mushrooms in a cooking dish with their can juices.

Combination microwave **Cook by microwave only.** Cover to cook and stir once, halfway through the cooking time. Leave to stand, covered, for 1–2 minutes before serving.

Quantity	Microwave Setting	Minutes
225 g (8 oz) frozen whole	High (100%)	5–6½
300 g (10½ oz) can whole	High (100%)	1½–1¾
300 g (10½ oz) can sliced	High (100%)	1½–1¾

Convection microwave and microwave only **Cook by microwave only.** Cover to cook and stir once, halfway through the cooking time. Leave to stand, covered, for 1–2 minutes before serving.

Quantity	Microwave Setting	Minutes
225 g (8 oz) frozen whole	High (100%)	4–5
300 g (10½ oz) can whole	High (100%)	1½
300 g (10½ oz) can sliced	High (100%)	1½

ONIONS

Fresh Whole and Sliced Onions

Peel and slice if liked. Place in a cooking dish with 30 ml (2 tbsp) water and a knob of butter (optional).

Combination microwave **Cook by microwave only.** Cover to cook and stir or rearrange once, halfway through the cooking time. Leave to stand for 2–5 minutes before serving.

Quantity	Microwave Setting	Minutes
450 g (1 lb) or 4 medium whole	High (100%)	10½–13
450 g (1 lb) sliced	High (100%)	7–10½

Convection microwave and microwave only **Cook by microwave only.** Cover to cook and stir or rearrange once, halfway through the cooking time. Leave to stand for 2–5 minutes before serving.

Quantity	Microwave Setting	Minutes
450 g (1 lb) or 4 medium whole	High (100%)	9–11
450 g (1 lb) sliced	High (100%)	6½–9

PARSNIPS

Fresh Whole and Sliced Parsnips

Peel and prick whole parsnips then slice if liked. Place in a shallow cooking dish with a knob of butter, 45 ml (3 tbsp) water and a dash of lemon juice.

***Combination microwave* Cook by microwave only.** Cover to cook and stir once, halfway through the cooking time. Leave to stand, covered, for 3 minutes before serving.

Quantity	Microwave Setting	Minutes
450 g (1 lb) whole	High (100%)	9½–13
450 g (1 lb) sliced	High (100%)	9–12

***Convection microwave and microwave only* Cook by microwave only.** Cover to cook and stir once, halfway through the cooking time. Leave to stand, covered, for 3 minutes before serving.

Quantity	Microwave Setting	Minutes
450 g (1 lb) whole	High (100%)	8–11
450 g (1 lb) sliced	High (100%)	8–10

Roast Parsnips

Peel and cut into sticks and toss in a little oil. Either add to a meat roast or roll in the fat juices for the last 20 minutes of the cooking time as below.

Combination microwave Preheat the oven, if necessary, according to the manufacturer's instructions. Turn over once, halfway through the cooking time.

Quantity	Temperature	Microwave Setting	Minutes
450 g (1 lb)	230°C	Low (30%)	18½

PEAS

Fresh and Frozen Peas

Weights refer to shelled weights of fresh peas. Place fresh or frozen shelled peas in a cooking dish with 45 ml (3 tbsp) water and a knob of butter if liked.

Combination microwave **Cook by microwave only.** Cover to cook and stir once, halfway through the cooking time. Leave to stand, covered, for 3–5 minutes before serving.

Quantity	Microwave Setting	Minutes
225 g (8 oz) fresh	High (100%)	3¾–5
450 g (1 lb) fresh	High (100%)	6½–8½
225 g (8 oz) frozen	High (100%)	3¾–6½
450 g (1 lb) frozen	High (100%)	6½–8½

Convection microwave and microwave only **Cook by microwave only.** Cover to cook and stir once, halfway through the cooking time. Leave to stand, covered, for 3–5 minutes before serving.

Quantity	Microwave Setting	Minutes
225 g (8 oz) fresh	High (100%)	3½–4
450 g (1 lb) fresh	High (100%)	5–7
225 g (8 oz) frozen	High (100%)	3½–5
450 g (1 lb) frozen	High (100%)	5–7

Canned Peas

Drain and place in a cooking dish with 30 ml (2 tbsp) of the can juices.

Combination microwave **Cook by microwave only.** Cover to cook and stir once, halfway through the cooking time.

Quantity	Microwave Setting	Minutes
425 g (15 oz) can	High (100%)	2–3

Convection microwave and microwave only **Cook by microwave only.** Cover to cook and stir once, halfway through the cooking time.

Quantity	Microwave Setting	Minutes
425 g (15 oz) can	High (100%)	1½–2½

PEPPERS

Stuffed Baked Peppers

Cut 4 peppers in half lengthways and remove the seeds. Blanch for a few minutes in boiling water then drain and fill with a cooked rice and meat, fish or poultry mixture. Place in a shallow dish and surround with 30 ml (2 tbsp) water.

Combination microwave Preheat the oven if necessary according to the manufacturer's instructions. Sprinkle with a little cheese towards the end of the cooking time if liked.

Quantity	Temperature	Microwave Setting	Minutes
4 medium	200°C	Medium (50%)	11–14

Convection microwave **Cook by convection only.** Preheat the oven for 10 minutes or according to the manufacturer's instructions. Sprinkle with a little cheese towards the end of the cooking time if liked.

Quantity	Convection Temperature	Minutes
4 medium	170°C	27–32

Microwave only Sprinkle with a little cheese towards the end of the cooking time if liked. Ideally blanch the peppers in the microwave before filling for 3–5 minutes at High (100%) to soften.

Quantity	Microwave Setting	Minutes
4 medium	High (100%)	2½–4 (if microwave blanched)
		4–6½ (if blanched in boiling water)

POTATOES

Boiled New Potatoes

Scrub and scrape if liked. Place in a cooking dish with 60 ml (4 tbsp) water.

Combination microwave **Cook by microwave only.** Cover to cook and stir once, halfway through the cooking time. Leave to stand, covered, for 5 minutes before serving.

Quantity	Microwave Setting	Minutes
450 g (1 lb)	High (100%)	6½–8½

Convection microwave and microwave only **Cook by microwave only.** Cover to cook and stir once, halfway through the cooking time. Leave to stand, covered, for 5 minutes before serving.

Quantity	Microwave Setting	Minutes
450 g (1 lb)	High (100%)	5–7

Creamed Potatoes

Peel the potatoes and dice into small cubes. Place in a cooking dish with 75 ml (3 fl oz) water.

Combination microwave **Cook by microwave only**. Cover to cook and stir once, halfway through the cooking time. Leave to stand, covered, for 5 minutes before draining and mashing with butter, cream and seasonings to taste.

Quantity	Microwave Setting	Minutes
1 kg (2 lb)	High (100%)	12–14

Convection microwave and microwave only **Cook by microwave only**. Cover to cook and stir once, halfway through the cooking time. Leave to stand, covered, for 5 minutes before draining and mashing with butter, cream and seasonings to taste.

Quantity	Microwave Setting	Minutes
1 kg (2 lb)	High (100%)	10–12

Jacket Baked Potatoes

Scrub the potatoes and prick their skins.

Combination microwave Preheat the oven, if necessary, according to the manufacturer's instructions. Brush the potato skins with a little oil and place on the oven rack.

Quantity	Temperature	Microwave Setting	Minutes
1 × 175 g (6 oz)	250°C	High (100%)	4–5
2 × 175 g (6 oz)	250°C	High (100%)	6½–7
3 × 175 g (6 oz)	250°C	High (100%)	8–11
5 × 175 g (6 oz)	250°C	High (100%)	12–14

Convection microwave Cook by microwave first then by convection to crisp the skins if liked.

Quantity	Microwave Setting/Time	Convection/Minutes
1 × 175 g (6 oz)	High (100%)/3½–5 minutes	250°C/5–10 minutes
2 × 175 g (6 oz)	High (100%)/5–7 minutes	250°C/5–10 minutes
3 × 175 g (6 oz)	High (100%)/7–11 minutes	250°C/5–10 minutes
4 × 175 g (6 oz)	High (100%)/11–14 minutes	250°C/5–10 minutes

Microwave only If cooking more than 2 potatoes then arrange in a ring pattern in the microwave. Leave to stand for 3–5 minutes before serving.

Quantity	Microwave Setting	Minutes
1 × 175 g (6 oz)	High (100%)	3½–5
2 × 175 g (6 oz)	High (100%)	5–7
3 × 175 g (6 oz)	High (100%)	7–11
4 × 175 g (6 oz)	High (100%)	11–14

Lyonnaise Potatoes

Brush a 20 cm (8 in) dish with a little melted butter. Slice 675 g (1½ lb) potatoes very thinly and layer in the dish with a little chopped onion and garlic with salt and pepper to taste. Pour over 200 ml (7 fl oz) milk.

Combination microwave Preheat the oven, if necessary, according to the manufacturer's instructions.

Quantity	Temperature	Microwave Setting	Minutes
1 recipe above	180°C	High (100%)	15–18½

Convection microwave Cover loosely and cook by microwave first. Remove the cover then cook by convection to crisp and brown.

Quantity	Microwave Setting/Time	Convection/Minutes
1 recipe above	High (100%)/13 minutes	250°C/5–10 minutes

Microwave only Cover loosely and cook for half of the time. Remove the cover to cook for the remaining time. Leave to stand for 5 minutes before serving. Brown and crisp under a preheated hot grill if liked.

Quantity	Microwave Setting	Minutes
1 recipe above	High (100%)	13–15

Roast Potatoes

Peel and quarter about 1 kg (2 lb) potatoes, rinse and dry well.

Combination microwave Preheat the oven if necessary according to the manufacturer's instructions. Brush the potatoes well with oil and place on the wire rack or in an ovenproof dish on the trivet. Turn over once, halfway through the cooking time.

Quantity	Temperature	Microwave Setting	Minutes
1 kg (2 lb)	250°C	Medium (50%)	21½

Convection microwave Place the potatoes in an ovenproof dish with 75 ml (5 tbsp) water and a pinch of salt. Cover and cook by microwave first, drain and toss in 60 ml (4 tbsp) oil. Preheat the oven if necessary for 10 minutes or according to the manufacturer's instructions then cook by convection. Turn over once, halfway through the cooking time. Drain on absorbent kitchen paper.

Quantity	Microwave Setting/Minutes	Convection Temperature/Minutes
1 kg (2 lb)	High (100%)/8 minutes	230°C/20–25 minutes

Microwave only Not suitable since the potatoes do not crisp and brown adequately.

Frozen Mashed Potato Nuggets

Best cooked from frozen.

Combination microwave Cook by microwave only. Cover for cooking and stir once, halfway through the cooking time. Fluff with a fork before serving.

Quantity	Microwave Setting	Minutes
1 portion 150 g/5 oz (13–15 nuggets)	High (100%)	3½
2 portions 300 g/11 oz (26–30 nuggets)	High (100%)	6–6½
3 portions 450 g/1 lb (42–45 nuggets)	High (100%)	8

Convection microwave and microwave only Cook by microwave only. Cover for cooking and stir once, halfway through the cooking time. Fluff with a fork before serving.

Quantity	Microwave Setting	Minutes
1 portion 150 g/5 oz (13–15 nuggets)	High (100%)	2½
2 portions 300 g/11 oz (26–30 nuggets)	High (100%)	4
3 portions 450 g/1 lb (42–45 nuggets)	High (100%)	6½

Fresh Mashed Potato from the Packet

Best cooked from frozen.

Combination microwave **Cook by microwave only.** Take out of packet; place in a bowl with the milk and cook uncovered, stirring halfway through the cooking time. Stir the mashed potato well, adding butter or margarine if liked. Leave to stand for 2 minutes before serving.

Quantity	Milk	Microwave Setting	Minutes
175 g (6 oz)	50 ml (2 fl oz)	High (100%)	6½
350 g (12 oz)	100 ml (4 fl oz)	High (100%)	10

Convection microwave and microwave only **Cook by microwave only.** Place in a bowl with the milk and cook uncovered, stirring halfway through the cooking time. Stir the mashed potato well, adding butter or margarine if liked. Leave to stand for 2 minutes before serving.

Quantity	Milk	Microwave Setting	Minutes
175 g (6 oz)	50 ml (2 fl oz)	High (100%)	4
350 g (12 oz)	100 ml (4 fl oz)	High (100%)	7

SPINACH

Fresh Spinach

Trim and chop or shred then rinse thoroughly in several changes of water. Place in dish with just the water clinging to the leaves.

Combination microwave **Cook by microwave only.** Cover for cooking and stir once, halfway through the cooking time. Leave to stand for 2 minutes before serving.

Quantity	Microwave Setting	Minutes
450 g (1 lb)	High (100%)	6½–8

Convection microwave and microwave only **Cook by microwave only.** Cover for cooking and stir once, halfway through the cooking time. Leave to stand for 2 minutes before serving.

Quantity	Microwave Setting	Minutes
450 g (1 lb)	High (100%)	5–7

Frozen and Canned Spinach

Place frozen block of spinach in a cooking dish without any extra water. Drain canned spinach and place in a cooking dish.

Combination microwave **Cook by microwave only.** Cover for cooking. Break up and stir frozen spinach twice during the cooking time. Stir canned spinach once, halfway through the cooking time.

Quantity	Microwave Setting	Minutes
275 g (10 oz) packet frozen	High (100%)	7–9½
270 g (9½ oz) can	High (100%)	1½–1¾
400 g (14 oz) can	High (100%)	3

Convection microwave and microwave only **Cook by microwave only.** Cover for cooking. Break up and stir frozen spinach twice during the cooking time. Stir canned spinach once, halfway through the cooking time.

Quantity	Microwave Setting	Minutes
275 g (10 oz) packet frozen	High (100%)	6–8
270 g (9½ oz) can	High (100%)	1½
400 g (14 oz) can	High (100%)	2½

SWEDE

Fresh and Frozen Cubed Swede

Peel and cut into 1 cm (½ in) cubes. Place fresh prepared or frozen cubed swede in a cooking dish with 30 ml (2 tbsp) water. Leave to stand for 4 minutes before draining to serve. Toss or mash with butter, cream and seasonings if liked.

Combination microwave **Cook by microwave only.** Cover for cooking and stir once, halfway through the cooking time.

Quantity	Microwave Setting	Minutes
450 g (1 lb) fresh	High (100%)	10½–13
450 g (1 lb) frozen	High (100%)	8½–10½

Convection microwave and microwave only. **Cook by microwave only.** Cover for cooking and stir once, halfway through the cooking time.

Quantity	Microwave Setting	Minutes
450 g (1 lb) fresh	High (100%)	9–11
450 g (1 lb) frozen	High (100%)	7–9

SWEETCORN KERNELS
Frozen and Canned Corn Kernels

Place the frozen or canned corn kernels in a cooking dish. Add 60 ml (4 tbsp) water to frozen kernels and 30 ml (2 tbsp) can juice to drained canned kernels. Creamed corn kernels should be placed in the dish without any additional ingredients.

Combination microwave. **Cook by microwave only.** Cover for cooking and stir once, halfway though the cooking time. Leave to stand, covered, for 2–3 minutes before serving.

Quantity	Microwave Setting	Minutes
450 g (1 lb) frozen	High (100%)	7–8½
298 g (10½ oz) canned kernels	High (100%)	2–3
340 g (12 oz) canned kernels	High (100%)	2½–3
340 g (12 oz) canned creamed	High (100%)	2½–3

Convection microwave and microwave only. **Cook by microwave only.** Cover for cooking and stir once, halfway through the cooking time. Leave to stand, covered, for 2–3 minutes before serving.

Quantity	Microwave Setting	Minutes
450 g (1 lb) frozen	High (100%)	6½–7
298 g (10½ oz) canned kernels	High (100%)	1½–2½
340 g (12 oz) canned kernels	High (100%)	2–2½
340 g (12 oz) canned creamed	High (100%)	2–2½

TOMATOES
Fresh Whole and Halved Tomatoes

Prick whole tomatoes or cut in half if liked. Place in a cooking dish and dot with butter. Season with salt, pepper and herbs if liked.

Combination microwave. **Cook by microwave only.** Time according to ripeness and end use.

Quantity	Microwave Setting	Minutes
1 medium	High (100%)	½–¾
4 medium	High (100%)	2–2½
4 beef tomatoes	High (100%)	3½–3¾

Convection microwave and microwave only. **Cook by microwave only.** Time according to ripeness and end use.

Quantity	Microwave Setting	Minutes
1 medium	High (100%)	½
4 medium	High (100%)	1¾–2¼
4 beef tomatoes	High (100%)	3–3½

TURNIPS

Fresh Whole, Sliced and Cubed

Peel then slice or cut into 1 cm (½ in) cubes if liked. Prick whole turnips with a fork. Place in a dish with 45 ml (3 tbsp) water and a knob of butter.

***Combination microwave* Cook by microwave only.** Cover for cooking and stir or rearrange once, halfway through the cooking time. Leave to stand, covered, for 3 minutes before serving.

Quantity	Microwave Setting	Minutes
450 g (1 lb) whole	High (100%)	15–17½
450 g (1 lb) sliced	High (100%)	11½–13
450 g (1 lb) cubed	High (100%)	13–15½

***Convection microwave and microwave only.* Cook by microwave only.** Cover for cooking and stir or rearrange once, halfway through the cooking time. Leave to stand, covered, for 3 minutes before serving.

Quantity	Microwave Setting	Minutes
450 g (1 lb) whole	High (100%)	13–15
450 g (1 lb) sliced	High (100%)	10–11
450 g (1 lb) cubed	High (100%)	11–13

PASTA AND RICE

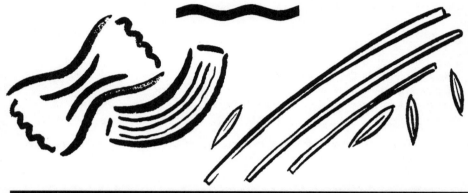

PASTA

To Cook Fresh Pasta

Place the pasta in a large cooking dish. Cover with 750 ml (1¼ pt) boiling water and add 5 ml (1 tsp) oil.

***Combination microwave* Cook by microwave only.** Cover loosely and stir once, halfway through the cooking time. Leave to stand for 2 minutes before draining to serve.

Quantity	Microwave Setting	Minutes
225 g (8 oz) egg noodles	High (100%)	1½–2½
225 g (8 oz) spaghetti	High (100%)	4–5
225 g (8 oz) tagliatelle	High (100%)	2½–3½
225 g (8 oz) ravioli	High (100%)	7–9

***Convection microwave and microwave only* Cook by microwave only.** Cover loosely and stir once, halfway though the cooking time. Leave to stand for 2 minutes before draining to serve.

Quantity	Microwave Setting	Minutes
225 g (8 oz) egg noodles	High (100%)	1½–2
225 g (8 oz) spaghetti	High (100%)	3½–5
225 g (8 oz) tagliatelle	High (100%)	1½–2½
225 g (8 oz) ravioli	High (100%)	5–7

To Cook Dried Pasta

Place the pasta in a large cooking dish. Add a generous 1.2 litres (2 pt) boiling water and 5 ml (1 tsp) oil.

Combination Microwave **Cook by microwave only.** Cover loosely and stir once, halfway through the cooking time. Leave to stand for 3–5 minutes before draining to serve.

Quantity	Microwave Setting	Minutes
225 g (8 oz) egg noodles	High (100%)	6½
225 g (8 oz) spaghetti	High (100%)	11–13
225 g (8 oz) tagliatelle	High (100%)	6½
225 g (8 oz) short-cut macaroni	High (100%)	10½
225 g (8 oz) pasta shapes	High (100%)	13
225 g (8 oz) ravioli	High (100%)	10½–11

Convection microwave and microwave only. **Cook by microwave only.** Cover loosely and stir once, halfway through the cooking time. Leave to stand for 3–5 minutes before draining to serve.

Quantity	Microwave Setting	Minutes
225 g (8 oz) egg noodles	High (100%)	5
225 g (8 oz) spaghetti	High (100%)	9–11
225 g (8 oz) tagliatelle	High (100%)	5
225 g (8 oz) short-cut macaroni	High (100%)	9
225 g (8 oz) pasta shapes	High (100%)	11–13
225 g (8 oz) ravioli	High (100%)	9

To Cook Canned Pasta

Place canned pasta in sauce (eg, macaroni cheese, ravioli in tomato sauce, spaghetti in tomato sauce) in a cooking dish.

Combination microwave **Cook by microwave only.** Cover and stir once, halfway through the cooking time.

Quantity	Microwave Setting	Minutes
213 g (7½ oz) can pasta in sauce	High (100%)	1½–1¾
397 g (14 oz) can pasta in sauce	High (100%)	2½–3
425 g (15 oz) can pasta in sauce	High (100%)	2½–3

Convection microwave and microwave only. **Cook by microwave only.** Cover and stir once, halfway through the cooking time.

Quantity	Microwave Setting	Minutes
213 g (7½ oz) can pasta in sauce	High (100%)	1¼–1½
397 g (14 oz) can pasta in sauce	High (100%)	2–2½
425 g (15 oz) can pasta in sauce	High (100%)	2–2½

Meat or Vegetable Homemade Lasagne

Make up the usual filling mixture for 4–6 people and layer with about 8 sheets of no-need-to-precook or easy-cook lasagne. Top with a little white or cheese sauce mixture.

Combination microwave Preheat the oven if necessary according to the manufacturer's instructions.

Quantity	Temperature	Microwave Setting	Minutes
to serve 4–6	200°C	Medium (50%)	22½–27

Convection microwave Preheat the oven if necessary for 10 minutes or according to the manufacturer's instructions. **Cook by convection first then by microwave.**

Quantity	Convection/Minutes	Microwave Setting/Time
to serve 4–6	200°C/20 minutes	Medium (50%)/4–9 minutes

Microwave only Leave to stand for 5 minutes after cooking before serving. Brown under a preheated hot grill until golden if liked.

Quantity	Microwave Setting	Minutes
to serve 4–6	Medium High (70%)	13–15

RICE

To Boil Long-Grain White and Brown Rice

Place the rice in a large cooking dish with the boiling water, a pinch of salt and a knob of butter if liked.

Combination microwave **Cook by microwave only.** Cover loosely to cook and cook on High (100%) for 3 minutes. Stir well, re-cover, reduce the power to Medium (50%) and cook for the remaining time, stirring once, Leave to stand, covered, for 5 minutes before serving. Fluff with a fork to serve.

Quantity Rice/Water	Microwave Setting	Minutes
100 g (4 oz) white rice/300 ml (½ pt)	Medium (50%)	11–13
100 g (4 oz) brown rice/300 ml (½ pt)	Medium (50%)	22½–25
225 g (8 oz) white rice/550 ml (18 fl oz)	Medium (50%)	11–13
225 g (8 oz) brown rice/550 ml (18 fl oz)	Medium (50%)	22½–25

Convection microwave and microwave only **Cook by microwave only.** Cover loosely to cook and cook on High (100%) for 3 minutes. Stir well, re-cover, reduce the power to Medium (50%) and cook for the remaining time, stirring once, Leave to stand, covered, for 5 minutes before serving. Fluff with a fork to serve.

Quantity Rice/Water	Microwave Setting	Minutes
100 g (4 oz) white rice/300 ml (½ pt)	Medium (50%)	11
100 g (4 oz) brown rice/300 ml (½ pt)	Medium (50%)	22½
225 g (8 oz) white rice/550 ml (18 fl oz)	Medium (50%)	11
225 g (8 oz) brown rice/550 ml (18 fl oz)	Medium (50%)	22½

To Boil Long-Grain and Wild Rice Mix

Place in a cooking dish with the boiling water, a pinch of salt and a knob of butter if liked.

***Combination microwave* Cook by microwave only**. Cover loosely to cook and cook on High (100%) for 3 minutes. Stir well, re-cover, reduce the power to Medium (50%) and cook for the remaining time, stirring once, Leave to stand, covered, for 5 minutes before serving. Fluff with a fork to serve.

Quantity Rice Mix/Water	Microwave Setting	Minutes
400 g (14 oz) pkt/700 ml (24 fl oz)	Medium (50%)	11–13

***Convection microwave and microwave only* Cook by microwave only**. Cover loosely to cook and cook on High (100%) for 2½ minutes. Stir well, re-cover, reduce the power to Medium (50%) and cook for the remaining time, stirring once. Leave to stand, covered, for 5 minutes before serving. Fluff with a fork to serve.

Quantity Rice Mix/Water	Microwave Setting	Minutes
400 g (14 oz) pkt/700 ml (24 fl oz)	Medium (50%)	11

Long Grain Rice In Sachets

Cook from frozen. Place unopened packets of rice or your own frozen rice into the oven (the sachets are self-venting) and cook for time stated.

***Combination microwave* Cook by microwave only.** Cook for time specified. Allow to stand for 1 minute then open sachet and serve.

Quantity	Microwave Setting	Minutes
1 × 200 g (7 oz) sachet	High (100%)	4½
2 × 200 g (7 oz) sachet	High (100%)	7
4 × 200 g (7 oz) sachet	High (100%)	12
6 × 200 g (7 oz) sachet	High (100%)	17

***Convection microwave and microwave only* Cook by microwave only.** Cook for time specified. Allow to stand for 1 minute then open sachet and serve.

Quantity	Microwave Setting	Minutes
1 × 200 g (7 oz) sachet	High (100%)	3½
2 × 200 g (7 oz) sachet	High (100%)	5
4 × 200 g (7 oz) sachet	High (100%)	9
6 × 200 g (7 oz) sachet	High (100%)	13

EGGS AND CHEESE

EGGS

Baked Eggs

Use either greased ramekin dishes, small greased cups or special microwave 6-holed bun or muffin trays to bake eggs. Crack an egg into each and quickly prick the yolk with the tip of a pointed knife.

Combination microwave **Cook by microwave only.** Cover loosely and rearrange dishes if possible halfway through the cooking time.

Quantity	Microwave Setting	Minutes
1	Medium (50%)	¾–1¼
2	Medium (50%)	1½–2
4	Medium (50%)	3½–3¾
6	Medium (50%)	6–6½

Convection microwave and microwave only **Cook by microwave only.** Cover loosely and rearrange the dishes if possible halfway through the cooking time.

Quantity	Microwave Setting	Minutes
1	Medium (50%)	¾–1
2	Medium (50%)	1½–1¾
4	Medium (50%)	3–3½
6	Medium (50%)	4½–5

Poached Eggs

Ideally cook in ramekin dishes or small teacups. Place 30 ml (2 tbsp) boiling water and a dash of vinegar into each ramekin or teacup. Carefully crack an egg into each.

***Combination microwave* Cook by microwave only.** Cover to cook. If cooking more than 2 eggs arrange in a ring pattern in the microwave. Rearrange once halfway through the cooking time. Leave to stand, covered, for 2–3 minutes before serving.

Quantity	Microwave Setting	Minutes
1	Medium (50%)	¾–1
2	Medium (50%)	1–1½
3	Medium (50%)	2½–3
4	Medium (50%)	3½–3¾

***Convection microwave and microwave only* Cook by microwave only.** Cover to cook. If cooking more than 2 eggs arrange in a ring pattern in the microwave. Rearrange once, halfway through the cooking time. Leave to stand, covered, for 2–3 minutes before serving.

Quantity	Microwave Setting	Minutes
1	Medium (50%)	½–¾
2	Medium (50%)	1–1¼
3	Medium (50%)	2–2½
4	Medium (50%)	3–3½

Scrambled Eggs

Crack eggs required into a bowl and add 15 ml (1 tbsp) milk per egg. Beat well to mix and season with salt and pepper to taste. If liked, melt a little butter in a cooking dish before adding the beaten egg mixture.

***Combination microwave* Cook by microwave only.** Stir halfway through the cooking time then twice during the standing time. Leave to stand for 1–2 minutes before serving.

Quantity	Microwave Setting	Minutes
1	High (100%)	¾–1
2	High (100%)	2¼–2¾
4	High (100%)	3–3½
6	High (100%)	3¾–4½
8	High (100%)	5–5¾

***Convection microwave and microwave only* Cook by microwave only.** Stir halfway through the cooking time then twice during the remaining time. Leave to stand for 1–2 minutes before serving.

Quantity	Microwave Setting	Minutes
1	High (100%)	¾–1
2	High (100%)	1¼–2
4	High (100%)	2–2½
6	High (100%)	3–3½
8	High (100%)	4–4½

CHEESE

Cheese Soufflé

Place 25 g (1 oz) butter in a bowl and microwave on High (100%) for 1 minute to melt. Stir in 25 g (1 oz) flour and blend well. Gradually add 200 ml (7 fl oz) milk and cook on High (100%) for 3 minutes, stirring every 1 minute until smooth, boiling and thickened. Beat in 100 g (4 oz) grated cheese with a little mustard and seasoning to taste. Stir in 4 egg yolks, blending well. Whisk 4 egg whites until they stand in stiff peaks and fold into the cheese mixture with a metal spoon. Pour into a buttered 1.2 litre (2 pt) soufflé dish and cook at once.

Combination microwave Preheat the oven according to the manufacturer's instruction. Serve at once.

Quantity	Temperature	Microwave Setting	Minutes
1 recipe above	250°C	High (100%)	6

Convection microwave Preheat the oven for 10 minutes or according to the manufacturer's instructions. **Cook by convection only.** Serve at once.

Quantity	Convection Temperature	Minutes
1 recipe above	190°C	20–22

Microwave only Not suitable since the soufflé does not crisp and brown adequately.

Variations

Mushroom Soufflé Add 100 g (4 oz) cooked chopped mushrooms instead of the cheese.
Smoked Fish Soufflé Add 100 g (4 oz) cooked chopped or flaked smoked fish instead of the cheese.
Cheesy Corn Soufflé Add 50 g (2 oz) cooked sweetcorn kernels to the cheese soufflé mixture.

SOFT CHEESES

To Soften or 'Ripen' Semi-Soft Chilled Cheese For Serving

Place on a serving dish. Check constantly during heating to ensure the cheese does not melt. Timings will depend upon temperature and the degree of ripeness of the cheese.

Combination microwave **Cook by microwave only.** Leave to stand for 5–10 minutes before serving.

Quantity	Microwave Setting	Minutes
225 g (8 oz)	Low (30%)	¼–¾

Convection microwave and microwave only **Cook by microwave only**. Leave to stand for 5–10 minutes before serving.

Quantity	Microwave Setting	Minutes
225 g (8 oz)	Low (30%)	¼–½

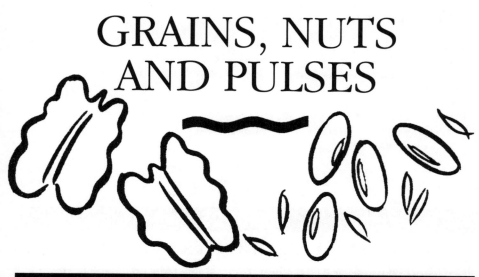

GRAINS, NUTS AND PULSES

GRAINS

Pot Barley, Bulghur or Cracked Wheat Grains, Pre-cooked Couscous, Millet Grains, Oat Grains, Rye Grains and Wheat Grains

Soak wheat and rye grains for 6–8 hours in cold water then drain. Toast barley, millet and oat grains if liked. Place in a cooking dish with the boiling water and a pinch of salt if liked. Add 50 g (2 oz) butter to the couscous mixture.

***Combination microwave* Cook by microwave only.** Cover loosely and cook all except couscous on High (100%) for 3 minutes. Reduce the power to Medium (50%) and cook for the remaining time. Leave to stand for 5–10 minutes before fluffing with a fork to serve.

Quantity Grain/Water	Microwave Setting	Minutes
175 g (6 oz) pot barley/1 litre (1¾ pt)	Medium (50%)	13–40
225 g (8 oz) bulghur/550 ml (18 fl oz)	Medium (50%)	9½–13
350 g (12 oz) couscous/250 ml (8 fl oz)	Medium (50%)	14–16½
225 g (8 oz) millet/650 ml (22 fl oz)	Medium (50%)	11–13
175 g (6 oz) oats/750 ml (1¼ pt)	Medium (50%)	18½–22½
175 g (6 oz) rye/750 ml (1¼ pt)	Medium (50%)	37–40
175 g (6 oz) wheat/1 litre (1¾ pt)	Medium (50%)	37–40

***Convection microwave* Cook by microwave only**. Cover loosely and cook all except couscous on High (100%) for 2½ minutes. Reduce the power to Medium (50%) and cook for the remaining time. Leave to stand for 5–10 minutes before fluffing with a fork to serve.

Quantity Grain/Water	Microwave Setting	Minutes
175 g (6 oz) pot barley/1 litre (1¾ pt)	Medium (50%)	37
225 g (8 oz) bulghur/550 ml (18 fl oz)	Medium (50%)	8–11
350 g (12 oz) couscous/250 ml (8 fl oz)	Medium (50%)	14
225 g (8 oz) millet/650 ml (22 fl oz)	Medium (50%)	11
175 g (6 oz) oats/750 ml (1¼ pt)	Medium (50%)	18½–21
175 g (6 oz) rye/750 ml (1¼ pt)	Medium (50%)	37
175 g (6 oz) wheat/1 litre (1¾ pt)	Medium (50%)	37

·NUTS·

ALMONDS

To Toast Whole and Flaked Almonds

Place blanched whole or flaked almonds in a single layer on a large heatproof plate.

***Combination microwave* Cook by microwave only**. Stir every 1 minute until golden. Allow to cool completely before storing.

Quantity	Microwave Setting	Minutes
50 g (2 oz) flaked	High (100%)	3–5
50 g (2 oz) whole	High (100%)	5–6½

***Convection microwave and microwave only* Cook by microwave only**. Stir every 1 minute until golden. Allow to cool completely before storing.

Quantity	Microwave Setting	Minutes
50 g (2 oz) flaked	High (100%)	2½–4
50 g (2 oz) whole	High (100%)	4–5

PEANUTS

Roasted Peanuts

Place shelled nuts on a large heatproof plate and add 5 ml (1 tsp) oil. Roll the nuts to coat in the oil.

Combination microwave **Cook by microwave only.** Stir twice during the cooking time. Drain on absorbent kitchen towel and toss in a little flavoured salt if liked after cooking.

Quantity	Microwave Setting	Minutes
150 g (5 oz)	High (100%)	5–7¼

Convection microwave and microwave only **Cook by microwave only.** Stir twice during the cooking time. Drain on absorbent kitchen towel and toss in a little flavoured salt if liked after cooking.

Quantity	Microwave Setting	Minutes
150 g (5 oz)	High (100%)	4–6½

·PULSES·

DRIED BEANS

Dried Aduki, Black, Blackeye, Borlotti, Broad, Butter, Cannellini, Flageolet, Haricot, Mung, Pinto, Red Kidney and Soya Beans

Soak dried beans overnight in cold water or hasten soaking by par-cooking in the microwave. (Place the dried beans in a cooking dish with boiling water to cover. Cover and cook on High/100% for 4 minutes. Leave to stand, covered, for 1½ hours before draining to cook.)

Combination microwave **Cook by microwave only.** Place soaked beans in a cooking dish and cover with boiling water. Cover and cook on High (100%) for 10½ minutes. Reduce the power setting and cook for times given below, adding extra boiling water to cover if needed. Drain and use as required.

Quantity	Microwave Setting	Minutes
225 g (8 oz) aduki, blackeye, mung and pinto beans	Medium (50%)	10½–16½
225 g (8 oz) black, borlotti, broad, butter, cannelloni, flageolet, haricot, red kidney and soya beans	Medium (50%)	21½–26

Convection microwave and microwave only Cook by microwave only. Place soaked beans in a cooking dish and cover with boiling water. Cover and cook on High (100%) for 9 minutes. Reduce the power setting and cook for the times given below, adding extra boiling water to cover if needed. Drain and use as required.

Quantity	Microwave Setting	Minutes
225 g (8 oz) aduki, blackeye, mung and pinto beans	Medium (50%)	9–14
225 g (8 oz) black, borlotti, broad, butter, cannelloni, flageolet, haricot, red kidney and soya beans	Medium (50%)	18½–22½

DRIED PEAS

Dried Chickpeas, Whole Green Peas and Split Peas

Soak dried peas overnight in cold water or according to the packet instructions.

Combination microwave Cook by microwave only. Place the soaked peas in a cooking dish and cover with boiling water. Cover and cook on High (100%) for 10½ minutes. Reduce the power setting and cook for the times given below, adding extra boiling water to cover if needed. Drain and use as required.

Quantity	Microwave Setting	Minutes
225 g (8 oz) chickpeas	Medium (50%)	21½–26
225 g (8 oz) whole green peas	Medium (50%)	10½–16½
225 g (8 oz) split peas	No extra cooking time needed	

Convection microwave and microwave only Cook by microwave only. Place the soaked peas in a cooking dish and cover with boiling water. Cover and cook on High (100%) for 9 minutes. Reduce the power setting and cook for the times given below, adding extra boiling water to cover if needed. Drain and use as required.

Quantity	Microwave Setting	Minutes
225 g (8 oz) chickpeas	Medium (50%)	18½–22½
225 g (8 oz) whole green peas	Medium (50%)	9–14
225 g (8 oz) split peas	No extra cooking time needed	

LENTILS

Dried Lentils

Place the lentils in a cooking dish with a few seasoning vegetables such as chopped onion, chopped celery, diced carrot or bouquet garni and squeeze of lemon juice. Add 900 ml (1½ pt) boiling water or stock.

Combination microwave **Cook by microwave only.** Cover for cooking and stir once, halfway through the cooking time. Cook for the shorter length of time if the lentils are to be served in a salad mixture or as a meal accompaniment, the longer time if the lentils are to be puréed for use.

Quantity	Microwave Setting	Minutes
225 g (8 oz)	High (100%)	16½–26

Convection microwave and microwave only **Cook by microwave only.** Cover for cooking and stir once, halfway through the cooking time. Cook for the shorter length of time if the lentils are to be served in a salad mixture or as a meal accompaniment, the longer time if the lentils are to be puréed for use.

Quantity	Microwave Setting	Minutes
225 g (8 oz)	High (100%)	14–22½

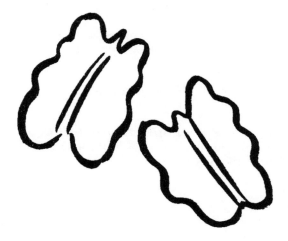

SAUCES

APPLE SAUCE

Peel, core and slice 450 g (1 lb) apples and place in a bowl with 15 ml (1 tbsp) water or fruit juice, a knob of butter and the juice of ½ lemon.

Combination microwave **Cook by microwave only.** Cover for cooking and stir once, halfway through the cooking time. Serve chunky or purée until smooth to serve.

Quantity	Microwave Setting	Minutes
1 recipe above	High (100%)	6½–8

Convection microwave and microwave only **Cook by microwave only.** Cover for cooking and stir once, halfway through the cooking time. Serve chunky or purée until smooth to serve.

Quantity	Microwave Setting	Minutes
1 recipe above	High (100%)	5–7

BÉARNAISE SAUCE

Place 4 egg yolks, 5 ml (1 tsp) grated onion, 5 ml (1 tsp) tarragon vinegar and 5 ml (1 tsp) dry white wine in a blender goblet. Place 100 g (4 oz) butter in a jug.

Combination microwave **Cook by microwave only.** Cook the butter as below then, with the blender set on its highest speed, add the melted butter in a slow stready stream, blending until the sauce is thick and creamy. Serve as soon as possible with steaks and vegetables.

Quantity	Microwave Setting	Minutes
100 g (4 oz) butter	High (100%)	1–1¾

Convection microwave and microwave only **Cook by microwave only.** Cook the butter as below then, with the blender set on its highest speed, add the melted butter in a slow steady stream, blending until the sauce is thick and creamy. Serve as soon as possible with steaks and vegetables.

Quantity	Microwave Setting	Minutes
100 g (4 oz) butter	High (100%)	¾–1¼

CRANBERRY SAUCE

Place 450 g (1 lb) prepared cranberries in a large bowl with 90 ml (6 tbsp) water or orange juice, 350 g (12 oz) granulated sugar and a little grated orange zest if liked.

Combination microwave **Cook by microwave only.** Cover for cooking and stir three times during cooking until very soft and pulpy.

Quantity	Microwave Setting	Minutes
1 recipe above	High (100%)	20½–21½

Convection microwave and microwave only **Cook by microwave only.** Cover for cooking and stir three times during cooking until very soft and pulpy.

Quantity	Microwave Setting	Minutes
1 recipe above	High (100%)	17–18½

CUSTARD SAUCE

Real Egg Custard Sauce

Place 600 ml (1 pt) milk in a large jug and cook on High (100%) for 3½–4½ minutes until very hot. Beat 4 egg yolks and 45 ml (3 tbsp) sugar together in a bowl. Gradually add the hot milk, blending well.

***Combination microwave* Cook by microwave only.** Cook as below, stirring every 1 minute until the custard is thick enough to coat the back of a wooden spoon but do not allow to overcook and curdle. Flavour with a little vanilla essence after cooking if liked.

Quantity	Microwave Setting	Minutes
600 ml (1 pt)	Medium (50%)	8–9

***Convection microwave and microwave only* Cook by microwave only.** Cook as below, stirring every 1 minute until the custard is thick enough to coat the back of a wooden spoon, but do not allow to overcook and curdle. Flavour with a little vanilla essence after cooking if liked.

Quantity	Microwave Setting	Minutes
600 ml (1 pt)	Medium High (70%)	4–5

GRAVY

Place 30 ml (2 tbsp) pan juices or meat drippings into a dish and stir in 15–30 ml (1–2 tbsp) plain flour.

Combination microwave **Cook by microwave only.** Cook the flour mixture on High (100%) for 1–3 minutes, depending upon how dark the resulting gravy needs to be (use the shorter time for light meats, the longer for dark meats), stirring once. Gradually add a generous 300 ml (½ pt) stock and cook as below, stirring every 1 minute.

Quantity	Microwave Setting	Minutes
1 recipe above	High (100%)	2–3

Convection microwave and microwave only **Cook by microwave only.** Cook the flour mixture on High (100%) for ¾-2½ minutes, depending upon how dark the resulting gravy needs to be (use the shorter time for light meats, the longer for dark meats), stirring once. Gradually add a generous 300 ml (½ pt) stock and cook as below, stirring every 1 minute.

Quantity	Microwave Setting	Minutes
1 recipe above	High (100%)	1½–2½

HOLLANDAISE SAUCE

Combination, convection and microwave only ovens Place 100 g (4 oz) butter in a large jug and cook for the 1st time and Power below. Whisk in 45 ml (3 tbsp) lemon juice, 2 egg yolks, a pinch of mustard powder or 1.25 ml (¼ tsp) prepared mustard and salt and pepper to taste. Cook for the 2nd time and Power below. Whisk and serve with fish, egg and vegetable dishes. Makes enough to serve 4.

Quantity	1st time/Power	2nd time/Power
1 recipe above	1¼ minutes/High (100%)	¾ minute/Medium (50%)

WHITE SAUCE

White Pouring Sauce

Place 25 g (1 oz) butter in a large jug and melt by **cooking on microwave only.**
High (100%) for ½–¾ minute. Stir in 25 g (1 oz) flour then gradually blend in
300 ml (½ pt) milk and salt and pepper to taste.

Combination microwave **Cook by microwave only.** Stir once every
minute of the cooking time until smooth and thickened.

Quantity	Microwave Setting	Minutes
1 recipe above	High (100%)	3½–4¼

Convection microwave and microwave only **Cook by microwave
only.** Stir once every minute of the cooking time until smooth and thickened.

Quantity	Microwave Setting	Minutes
1 recipe above	High (100%)	3–3½

Variations

Basic White Coating Sauce Prepare and cook as above but use 50 g (2 oz)
butter (melt by **cooking on microwave only** on High (100%) for ¾–1 minute)
and 50 g (2 oz) flour with 300 ml (½ pt) milk with seasonings to taste.
Caper Sauce Add 30 ml (2 tbsp) chopped capers and 10 ml (2 tsp) caper
vinegar and stir well to blend.
Cheese Sauce Stir in 75 g (3 oz) grated cheese and a pinch of mustard until
melted and well blended.
Lemon Sauce Add the finely grated rind of 1 lemon and 15 ml (1 tbsp) lemon
juice and stir well to blend.
Mushroom Sauce Add 75g (3 oz) finely chopped cooked mushrooms and stir
well to blend.
Onion Sauce Add 1 large chopped and cooked onion and stir well to blend.
Parsley Sauce Add 15 ml (1 tbsp) chopped fresh parsley and stir well to blend.
Seafood Sauce Add 50 g (2 oz) finely chopped prawns or shrimps, a pinch of
dry mustard powder, a dash of anchovy essence and 10 ml (2 tsp) of lemon
juice and stir well to blend.

FRUIT AND BASIC PUDDINGS

·FRUIT·

APPLES

Baked Apples

Wash and core the apples and score a cut around the circumference of each to prevent bursting during cooking. Fill the centres with a little dried fruit, sugar or honey and butter if liked and surround with about 120 ml (4 fl oz) water or fruit juice. Leave to stand for 5 minutes before serving.

***Combination microwave* Cook by microwave only.** Rearrange once during the cooking time.

Quantity	Microwave Setting	Minutes
4 large	High (100%)	9½–10½

***Convection microwave and microwave only* Cook by microwave only.** Rearrange once during the cooking time.

Quantity	Microwave Setting	Minutes
4 large	High (100%)	8–9

Stewed Apples

Wash, peel, core and slice the apples and place in a cooking dish with 100 g (4 oz) sugar.

Combination microwave **Cook by microwave only.** Cover for cooking and stir once, halfway through the cooking time.

Quantity	Microwave Setting	Minutes
450 g (1 lb)	High (100%)	6½–8

Convection microwave and microwave only **Cook by microwave only.** Cover for cooking and stir once, halfway through the cooking time.

Quantity	Microwave Setting	Minutes
450 g (1 lb)	High (100%)	5–7

BANANAS

Baked Halved Bananas

Peel and halve the bananas lengthwise and place in a shallow cooking dish with a sprinkling of sugar and 30 ml (2 tbsp) fruit juice or favourite liqueur.

Combination microwave **Cook by microwave only.** Rearrange the halves twice during the cooking time to ensure they cook evenly. Leave to stand for 1–2 minutes before serving.

Quantity	Microwave Setting	Minutes
2 large, halved	High (100%)	3–4

Convection microwave and microwave only **Cook by microwave only.** Rearrange the halves twice during the cooking time to ensure they cook evenly. Leave to stand for 1–2 minutes before serving.

Quantity	Microwave Setting	Minutes
2 large, halved	High (100%)	2½–3½

BLACKCURRANTS AND REDCURRANTS
Fresh and Frozen

Top and tail fresh blackcurrants or redcurrants. Place fresh or frozen blackcurrants or redcurrants in a cooking dish with 30 ml (2 tbsp) water or fruit juice and 100 g (4 oz) sugar, mixing well.

Combination microwave **Cook by microwave only.** Cover to cook and stir once, halfway through the cooking time. Leave to stand, covered, for 5 minutes before serving or using.

Quantity	Microwave Setting	Minutes
450 g (1 lb) fresh	High (100%)	5
450 g (1 lb) frozen	High (100%)	3¾–6½

Convection microwave and microwave only **Cook by microwave only.** Cover to cook and stir once, halfway through the cooking time. Leave to stand, covered, for 5 minutes before serving or using.

Quantity	Microwave Setting	Minutes
450 g (1 lb) fresh	High (100%)	4
450 g (1 lb) frozen	High (100%)	3½–5

DAMSONS AND PLUMS
Stewed Fresh Damsons and Plums

Halve and stone. Place in a cooking dish with sugar to taste (about 100 g [4 oz]).

Combination microwave **Cook by microwave only.** Cover to cook and stir once, halfway through the cooking time. Leave to stand, covered, for 3–5 minutes before serving.

Quantity	Microwave Setting	Minutes
450 g (1 lb)	High (100%)	4–5

Convection microwave and microwave only **Cook by microwave only.** Cover to cook and stir once, halfway through the cooking time. Leave to stand, covered, for 3–5 minutes before serving.

Quantity	Microwave Setting	Minutes
450 g (1 lb)	High (100%)	3½–4

GOOSEBERRIES
Stewed Gooseberries

Place fresh or thawed frozen gooseberries in a cooking dish with 30 ml (2 tbsp) water.

***Combination microwave* Cook by microwave only.** Cover to cook and stir once, halfway through the cooking time. Add 100 g (4 oz) sugar (or sugar to taste) and mix well. Leave to stand, covered, for 5 minutes before serving or puréeing for use.

Quantity	Microwave Setting	Minutes
450 g (1 lb)	High (100%)	4–6½

***Convection microwave or microwave only* Cook by microwave only.** Cover to cook and stir once, halfway through the cooking time. Add 100 g (4 oz) sugar (or sugar to taste) and mix well. Leave to stand, covered, for 5 minutes before serving or puréeing for use.

Quantity	Microwave Setting	Minutes
450 g (1 lb)	High (100%)	3½–5

PEACHES
Poached Peaches

Place 4 whole or 4 sliced skinned peaches in a cooking dish with 300 ml (½ pt) hot sugar syrup. If using whole peaches then prick before cooking.

***Combination microwave* Cook by microwave only.** Cover loosely to cook and stir or rearrange once, halfway through the cooking time. Leave to stand, covered, for 5 minutes before serving or allow to cool then chill.

Quantity	Microwave Setting	Minutes
4 whole peaches	High (100%)	3¾–4
4 sliced peaches	High (100%)	3

***Convection microwave and microwave only* Cook by microwave only.** Cover loosely to cook and stir or rearrange once, halfway through the cooking time. Leave to stand, covered, for 5 minutes before serving or allow to cool then chill.

Quantity	Microwave Setting	Minutes
4 whole peaches	High (100%)	3½
4 sliced peaches	High (100%)	2½

PEARS

Poached Whole Pears

Peel whole pears, keeping the stalks intact. Place in a cooking dish with 300 ml (½ pt) sugar syrup or red wine syrup.

***Combination microwave* Cook by microwave only.** Cover loosely to cook and rearrange once, halfway through the cooking time. Leave to stand, covered, for 5 minutes before serving hot or leave until cold then chill.

Quantity	Microwave Setting	Minutes
1 kg (2 lb) cooking pears	High (100%)	10½
1 kg (2 lb) dessert pears	High (100%)	5

***Convection microwave and microwave only* Cook by microwave only.** Cover loosely to cook and rearrange once, halfway through the cooking time. Leave to stand, covered, for 5 minutes before serving hot or leave until cold then chill.

Quantity	Microwave Setting	Minutes
1 kg (2 lb) cooking pears	High (100%)	9
1 kg (2 lb) dessert pears	High (100%)	4

Pastry-wrapped Pear Dumplings

Roll out 350 g (12 oz) puff pastry and cut into thin strips. Peel 6 dessert pears and core from the base, leaving the pears whole. Stuff the pears with a little sugar and liqueur if liked. Carefully wind the pastry strips around the pears, overlapping slightly as you go and secure each new strip with a little water – the finished pears should have a beehive-like appearance. Glaze with beaten egg and place on a cooking dish.

Combination microwave Preheat the oven, if necessary, according to the manufacturer's instructions. Cook until golden and the pears are tender; test by inserting a skewer.

Quantity	Temperature	Microwave Setting	Minutes
1 recipe above	200°C	Medium (50%)	18½–22½

Convection microwave **Cook by convection only.** Preheat the oven for 10 minutes or according to the manufacturer's instructions. Cook until golden and the pears are tender; test by inserting a skewer.

Quantity	Convection Temperature	Minutes
1 recipe above	200°C	27–37

Microwave only Not suitable since the pastry does not crisp and brown adequately.

RHUBARB

Fresh Stewed Rhubarb

Trim and cut into small lengths. Place in a cooking dish with 30 ml (2 tbsp) water.

Combination microwave **Cook by microwave only.** Cover to cook and stir once, halfway through the cooking time. After cooking, stir in sugar to taste and leave to stand for 3 minutes before serving or using.

Quantity	Microwave Setting	Minutes
450 g (1 lb)	High (100%)	7–8

Convection microwave and microwave only **Cook by microwave only.** Cover to cook and stir once, halfway through the cooking time. After cooking, stir in sugar to taste and leave to stand for 3 minutes before serving or using.

Quantity	Microwave Setting	Minutes
450 g (1 lb)	High (100%)	6–6¾

·BASIC PUDDINGS·

APPLE PIE

Thaw 1 (368 g [13 oz]) packet frozen shortcrust pastry. Line the base of a 23 cm (9 in) ovenproof glass pie plate with half of the pastry. Top with 675 g (1½ lb) lightly cooked and sweetened sliced apples. Cover with the remaining pastry. Glaze with beaten egg and sprinkle with caster sugar.

Combination microwave Preheat the oven if necessary according to the manufacturer's instructions.

Quantity	Temperature	Microwave Setting	Minutes
1 recipe above	200°C	Medium (50%)	18½–22½

Convection microwave **Cook by convection only.** Preheat the oven for 10 minutes or according to the manufacturer's instructions.

Quantity	Convection Temperature	Minutes
1 recipe above	220°C	25

Microwave only Not suitable since the pastry does not brown and crisp adequately.

BASIC SPONGE PUDDING

Cream 175 g (6 oz) butter with 175 g (6 oz) caster sugar until pale and fluffy. Beat in 3 eggs then fold in 175 g (6 oz) self-raising flour and 60 ml (4 tbsp) milk to make a mixture with a soft dropping consistency. Lightly butter a 1.2 litre (2 pt) pudding basin and, for easy release, coat with a few crushed biscuit crumbs. Spoon in the mixture.

Combination microwave **Cook by microwave only.** Rotate the basin every 2 minutes if necessary to ensure even rising. Leave to stand for 2 minutes before turning out to serve.

Quantity	Microwave Setting	Minutes
1 recipe above	Medium (50%)	12–14
	OR High (100%)	6–6½

Convection microwave and microwave only **Cook by microwave only.** Rotate the basin every 2 minutes if necessary to ensure even rising. Leave to stand for 2 minutes before turning out to serve.

Quantity	Microwave Setting	Minutes
1 recipe above	Medium High (70%)	7

BREAD AND BUTTER PUDDING

Spread 4 large or 6 medium bread slices with 50 g (2 oz) butter and cut each into quarters. Arrange in a 1.2 litre (2 pt) pie dish, sprinkling between each layer with 50 g (2 oz) sultanas. Beat 450 ml (¾ pt) milk with 3 eggs and 40 g (1½ oz) sugar and pour over the bread mixture. Leave to stand for 20 minutes to soak in.

Combination microwave Preheat the oven if necessary according to the manufacturer's instructions.

Quantity	Temperature	Microwave Setting	Minutes
1 recipe above	220°C	Medium (50%)	13

Convection microwave **Cook by convection only.** Preheat the oven for 10 minutes or according to the manufacturer's instructions.

Quantity	Convection Temperature	Minutes
1 recipe above	200°C	45

Microwave only Place the prepared bread and butter pudding in a shallow waterbath in the microwave. Cook for the time below but allow a 5 minute standing time halfway through the cooking time. The bread and butter pudding is cooked when the custard sets in the centre. Crisp under a preheated hot grill before serving if liked.

Quantity	Convection Temperature	Minutes
1 recipe above	High (100%)	9

CHRISTMAS PUDDING

To Cook a Favourite Christmas Pudding Mixture

Make up your favourite Christmas pudding mixture, remembering that darker mixtures produce better results. Also add a little more liquid, say 15 ml (1 tbsp) more than usual to give good moist results. Place in a 1.2 litre (2 pt) greased pudding basin. Ideally store the cooked pudding for 1 month to mature before reheating to serve.

Combination microwave **Cook by microwave only.** Cover loosely and leave to stand, covered, for 15 minutes before serving. Alternatively allow to cool before wrapping to store.

Quantity	Microwave Setting	Minutes
1.2 litre (2 pt) pudding	High (100%)	8½
	OR Low (30%)	OR 20½–25

Convection microwave and microwave only **Cook by microwave only.** Cover loosely and leave to stand, covered, for 15 minutes before serving. Alternatively allow to cool before wrapping to store.

Quantity	Microwave Setting	Minutes
1.2 litre (2 pt) pudding	High (100%)	7
	OR Low (30%)	OR 17–22

To Reheat Cooked Christmas Pudding

Pour a little brandy over the pudding before cooking, if liked, to moisten.

Combination microwave **Cook by microwave only.** Cover loosely and leave to stand for 3–4 minutes before serving.

Quantity	Microwave Setting	Minutes
1.2 litre (2 pt) pudding	High (100%)	2–3

Convection microwave and microwave only **Cook by microwave only.** Cover loosely and leave to stand for 3–4 minutes before serving.

Quantity	Microwave Setting	Minutes
1.2 litre (2 pt) pudding	High (100%)	1½–2½

EVE'S PUDDING

Peel, core and slice a generous 450 g (1 lb) apples into a cooking dish and sprinkle with sugar to taste. Beat 50 g (2 oz) butter or margarine with 50 g (2 oz) sugar, 1 egg, 50 g (2 oz) self-raising flour and 15 ml (1 tbsp) milk. Spread over the apples.

Combination microwave Preheat the oven if necessary according to the manufacturer's instructions. Serve hot with custard or cream.

Quantity	Temperature	Microwave Setting	Minutes
1 recipe above	200°C	Low (30%)	14

Convection microwave Preheat the oven for 10 minutes or according to the manufacturer's instructions. **Cook by convection first then by microwave.** Serve hot with custard or cream.

Quantity	Convection Temperature/Minutes	Microwave Setting/Time
1 recipe above	200°C/30 minutes	Medium (50%)/3½ minutes

Microwave only Best results are obtained here if the sponge topping is doubled in quantity. Brown under a preheated hot grill before serving if liked.

Quantity	Microwave Setting	Minutes
1 recipe above with double topping	Medium High (70%)	11

FRUIT CRUMBLE

Place 900 g (2 lb) prepared fruit in a dish with sugar or honey to taste. Add spices if liked. Make a crumble mixture by rubbing 75 g (3 oz) butter into 175 g (6 oz) flour then stir in 75 g (3 oz) sugar. Sprinkle over the fruit mixture.

Combination microwave Preheat oven if necessary according to manufacturer's instructions.

Quantity	Temperature	Microwave Setting	Minutes
1 recipe above	200°C	Low (30%)	18½–21

Convection microwave Either **cook by convection first then microwave** or **by microwave only** (see instructions below). Preheat the oven for 10 minutes or according to manufacturer's instructions. Leave to stand for 5 minutes before serving.

Quantity	Convection/Minutes	Microwave Setting/Minutes
1 recipe above	220°C/10 minutes	High (100%)/8–10

Microwave only Leave to stand for 5 minutes before serving. Brown under a preheated hot grill if liked.

Quantity	Microwave Setting	Minutes
1 recipe above	High (100%)	13–15

JAM ROLY POLY

Sift 225 g (8 oz) self-raising flour with a pinch of salt. Stir in 100 g (4 oz) shredded suet and about 150 ml (¼ pt) water to make a soft and pliable dough. Knead until smooth and roll out to a rectangle measuring 23 × 30 cm (9 × 12 in). Spread with about 90 ml (6 tbsp) jam, almost to the edges. Roll up the pastry from one of the short ends and seal the edges to enclose the jam filling.

Combination microwave Preheat the oven if necessary according to the manufacturer's instructions. Place on an ovenproof plate or flan dish and sprinkle with a little caster sugar if liked.

Quantity	Temperature	Microwave Setting	Minutes
1 recipe above	200°C	Medium (50%)	13–15

Convection microwave Preheat the oven for 10 minutes or according to the manufacturer's instruction. Place on an ovenproof plate or flan dish and sprinkle with a little caster sugar if liked. **Cook by convection first then by microwave.**

Quantity	Convection/Minutes	Microwave setting/Time
1 recipe above	200°C/40 minutes	Medium High (70%)/1½ minutes

Microwave only Place on a lightly greased dish and sprinkle with a little caster sugar if liked. Brown under a preheated hot grill after cooking if desired.

Quantity	Microwave Setting	Minutes
1 recipe above	High (100%)	4–5

BREAD, CAKES, AND SWEETS

BREAD

Wholemeal Bread

Separate recipes have been given here for combination microwave, convection microwave and microwave only ovens since there are ideal quantities and shapes to cook in each oven.

Combination microwave Sift 675 g (1½ lb) plain wholemeal flour (or half wholemeal and half granary flour) with 5 ml (1 tsp) salt. Rub in 25 g (1 oz) butter and 25 g (1 oz) lard. Stir in 1 sachet of easy blend dried yeast. Add 400 ml (14 fl oz) warm water or water and milk mixed and mix well. Knead until smooth and elastic. Place in an oiled bowl and leave to prove until doubled in size. Knock back and knead for a further 5 minutes. Divide and shape into 3 loaves to fit 3 small greased loaf dishes. Brush with a little water and sprinkle with seeds if liked. Preheat the oven, if necessary, according to the manufacturer's instructions. The loaves are cooked when well-risen, golden and the bases sound hollow when tapped on the bottom with the knuckles. Cool on a wire rack.

Quantity	Temperature	Microwave Setting	Minutes
1 recipe above	220°C	Low (30%)	14–18½

Convection microwave **Cook by convection only.** Place 675 g (1½ lb) wholemeal flour in a bowl and cook on High (100%) for 1 minute. Rub in 15 g (½ oz) lard and add 5 ml (1 tsp) salt. Sprinkle 15 g (½ oz) dried yeast over 150 ml (¼ pt) warm water into which 5 ml (1 tsp) sugar has been dissolved. Leave in a warm place until frothy, about 10–15 minutes. Add to the flour mixture with a further 300 ml (½ pt) warm water and mix well. Knead until smooth and elastic. Place in an oiled bowl and leave to prove until doubled in size. Knock back and knead for a further 5 minutes. Divide and shape into 2 loaves and place in 2 greased 1 kg (2 lb) loaf tins. Leave in a warm place until the dough has doubled in size. Brush with a little water and sprinkle with seeds if liked. Preheat the oven for 10 minutes or according to the manufacturer's instructions. The loaves are cooked when well-risen, golden and the bases sound hollow when tapped on the bottom with the knuckles. Cool on a wire rack.

Quantity	Convection Temperature	Minutes
1 recipe above	220°C	20

Microwave only Sift 225 g (8 oz) wholemeal flour and 225 g (8 oz) plain white flour into a bowl with 5 ml (1 tsp) salt. Rub in 40 g (1½ oz) butter. Sprinkle 5 ml (1 tsp) dried yeast over 150 ml (¼ pt) warm water into which 5 ml (1 tsp) sugar has been dissolved. Leave in a warm place until frothy, about 10–15 minutes. Add to the flour mixture with a further 150 ml (¼ pt) warm water and mix well. Knead until smooth and elastic. Place in an oiled bowl and leave to prove until doubled in size. Knock back and knead for a further 5 minutes. Shape to fit a 15 cm (6 in) greased soufflé dish or a 900 g (2 lb) loaf dish lined with greaseproof paper. Leave in a warm place until the dough has doubled in size. Brush with a little water and sprinkle with seeds if liked. The loaf is cooked when well-risen and the base sounds hollow when tapped on the bottom with the knuckles. Leave to stand in the dish for 10 minutes before turning out to cool on a wire rack. Brown the top under a preheated hot grill if liked.

Quantity	Microwave Setting	Minutes
1 recipe above	High (100%)	4

WHITE BREAD

Combination microwave Follow the instructions for making wholemeal bread (see previous page) but use strong plain white flour instead of wholemeal flour. Glaze with beaten egg if liked and sprinkle with nibbed wheat.

Quantity	Temperature	Microwave Setting	Minutes
1 recipe	220°C	Low (30%)	14–18½

Convection microwave Follow the instructions for making wholemeal bread but use strong plain white flour instead of wholemeal flour. Glaze with beaten egg if liked and sprinkle with nibbed wheat.

Quantity	Convection Temperature	Minutes
1 recipe	220°C	20

Microwave only Follow the instructions for making wholemeal bread but replace all the wholemeal flour with strong plain white flour. Brush with a little water and sprinkle with nibbed wheat if liked. Brown under a preheated hot grill until golden, if liked, after cooking.

Quantity	Microwave Setting	Minutes
1 recipe	High (100%)	4

·CAKES·

FAIRY CAKES

Cream 75 g (3 oz) butter with 75 g (3 oz) caster sugar until light and fluffy. Beat in 2 small eggs then fold in 75 g (3 oz) self-raising flour. Divide evenly between 12 paper bun cases and place in a suitable baking tin or dish (see manufacturer's information). After cooking allow to cool on a wire rack.

Combination and convection microwave Cook by convection only. Preheat the oven if necessary according to the manufacturer's instructions.

Quantity	Convection Temperature	Minutes
12	180°C	15

Microwave only Spoon the mixture into double-thickness paper bun cases. Place in a six-holed bun tray or muffin pan. Cook 6 buns at a time, rearranging the buns once halfway through the cooking time. Repeat with the remaining mixture.

Quantity	Microwave Setting	Minutes
per 6 cakes	High (100%)	1½–2

Variations

Butterfly Cakes Remove a small slice from the top of each cake and cut in half (for wings). Pipe the top of each cake with a little buttercream. Replace the wings and dust lightly with icing sugar.
Cherry Cakes Stir 40 g (1½ oz) chopped glacé cherries into the basic mixture.
Chocolate Chip Fairy Cakes Stir 40 g (1½ oz) chocolate chips or polka dots into the basic mixture.
Queen Cakes Stir 40 g (1½ oz) currants into the basic mixture.

MADEIRA CAKE

Cream 175 g (6 oz) butter with 175 g (6 oz) caster sugar and the finely grated zest of 1 lemon until light and fluffy. Beat in 3 eggs, a little at a time, blending well. Sift 225 g (8 oz) plain flour with 7.5 ml (1½ tsp) baking powder and fold into the creamed mixture. Add 30 ml (2 tbsp) milk if the mixture seems to be too stiff.

Combination microwave Preheat the oven if necessary according to the manufacturer's instructions. Spoon into an 18 cm (7 in) round cake tin or ovenproof glass cake dish and level the surface. Top with a piece of citron peel if liked. Allow to cool slightly before turning out on to a wire rack to cool.

Quantity	Temperature	Microwave Setting	Minutes
1 recipe above	230°C	Low (30%)	14

Convection microwave Preheat the oven for 10 minutes or according to the manufacturer's instructions. Spoon the mixture into an 18 cm (7 in) round cake tin or ovenproof glass dish and level the surface. Top with a piece of citron peel if liked. Cook by convection first then by microwave. Allow to cool slightly before turning out on to a wire rack to cool.

Quantity	Convection/Minutes	Microwave Setting/Time
1 recipe above	180°C/45 minutes	Medium (50%)/3½ minutes

Microwave only Spoon into an 18 cm (7 in) ovenproof cake dish and level the surface. Top with a piece of citron peel if liked. Cook for the first microwave power level and time then increase the power level and cook for the second time. Allow to cool slightly before turning out on to a wire rack to cool.

Quantity	1st Microwave Setting/Time	2nd Microwave Setting/Time
1 recipe above	Medium (50%)/9 minutes	High (100%)/¾ minute

Variation

Caraway Seed Cake Prepare and cook the cake mixture above but add 15 ml (3 tsp) caraway seeds to the basic mixture and omit the strip of citron peel (if used).

RICH FRUIT CAKE

Small and large fruit cakes can be successfully cooked in the combination and convection microwave but it is often difficult to achieve good results with the microwave only. A standard 20 cm (8 in) deep round rich fruit cake recipe has therefore been given for the combination and convection microwave and a specially developed 18 cm (7 in) less-rich fruit cake recipe has been given for the microwave only to ensure success in all ovens.

Combination microwave Cream 275 g (10 oz) butter with 275 g (10 oz) brown sugar until light and fluffy. Beat in a little grated lemon rind and 5 beaten eggs. Sift 350 g (12 oz) plain flour with 5 ml (1 tsp) ground mixed spice and 2.5 ml (½ tsp) bicarbonate of soda. Fold into the creamed mixture with 1 kg (2¼ lb) mixed dried fruit, 75 g (3 oz) glacé cherries and 75 g (3 oz) ground or slivered almonds. Add a generous splash of sherry or brandy and 15 ml (1 tbsp) black treacle and mix well. Line the base and sides of a 20 cm (8 in) deep round cake tin (if your model of microwave allows metal) or dish with greaseproof paper. Spoon in the prepared mixture and make a slight hollow in the centre to allow the cake to rise evenly. Test to see if the cake is cooked by inserting a wooden cocktail stick or skewer – if it comes out clean the cake is cooked. Allow to cool slightly after cooking before turning out on to a wire rack to cool further. Store in an airtight tin for 1 month before eating.

Quantity	Temperature	Microwave Setting	Hours
1 recipe above	140°C	Low (30%)	1¼–1¾

Convection microwave Use exactly the same mixture as for the Combination Microwave. Line a 20 cm (8 in) deep cake tin with greaseproof paper and surround the outside of the tin with brown paper, secured with string. Spoon in the prepared mixture and make a slight hollow in the centre to allow the cake to rise evenly. **Cook by convection first then by microwave.**

Quantity	Convection/Hours	Microwave Setting/Time
1 recipe above	150°C/2–2¼ hours	Medium (50%)/3½ minutes

Microwave only Mix 2 eggs with 30 ml (2 tbsp) black treacle, 175 g (6 oz) dark soft brown sugar and 37 ml (2½ tbsp) oil. Sift 175 g (6 oz) self-raising flour with 2.5 ml (½ tsp) salt and 5 ml (1 tsp) ground mixed spice. Fold into the oil mixture with 150 ml (¼ pt) milk. Add 450 g (1 lb) mixed dried fruit, 75 g (3 oz) glacé cherries, 50 g (2 oz) slivered almonds and 75 g (3 oz) chopped mixed peel, mixing well. Lightly grease an 18 cm (7 in) deep dish and line the base with a disc of greaseproof paper. Add the prepared mixture and level the surface. Test to see if the cake is cooked by inserting a wooden cocktail stick or skewer – if it comes out clean the cake is cooked. Leave to stand in the dish for 30–40 minutes before turning out to cool on a wire rack. Store in an airtight tin for 1 week to mature before eating.

Quantity	Microwave Setting	Minutes
1 recipe above	Low (30%)	49–63

VICTORIA SANDWICH CAKE

Cream 175 g (6 oz) butter or margarine with 175 g (6 oz) caster sugar until light and fluffy. Beat in 3 eggs, alternately with 175 g (6 oz) self-raising flour and 30 ml (2 tbsp) milk. When cooked sandwich the split cake or layers with jam and cream if liked and dust the top with sifted icing sugar.

Combination microwave Preheat the oven if necessary according to the manufacturer's instructions. Grease and line the base of a 20 cm (8 in) deep round cake dish with greaseproof paper. Spoon in the cake mixture and smooth the surface, making a small hollow in the centre of the mixture. The cake is cooked when browned and the top springs back when lightly touched with the fingertips. Leave to stand for 5–10 minutes before turning out to cool on a wire rack.

Quantity	Temperature	Microwave Setting	Minutes
20 cm (8 in) cake	200°C	Low (30%)	14

Convection microwave **Cook by convection only.** Preheat the oven for 10 minutes or according to the manufacturer's instructions. Divide the mixture between 2 greased 18 cm (7 in) sandwich tins. Place one sandwich on the base or turntable and the other on the baking trivet. The cakes are cooked when the tops are golden and spring back when lightly touched with the fingertips. Turn out to cool on wire racks.

Quantity	Convection Temperature	Minutes
2 × 20 cm (8 in) sandwich cakes	180°C	30

Microwave only Line a 20 cm (8 in) deep cake dish with microwave cling film, or grease and line with greaseproof paper. Spoon the filling into the dish and level the surface. The cake is cooked when the top still appears slightly tacky but the sponge underneath is firm to the touch. Leave to stand for 5 minutes before turning out to cool on a wire rack (the cake will finish cooking during this standing time and the top will dry).

Quantity	Microwave Setting	Minutes
20 cm (8 in) cake	High (100%)	6–6¾

·SWEETS·

BAKEWELL TART

Roll out 175 g (6 oz) shortcrust pastry and use to line a 20 cm (8 in) flan dish. Spread 45 ml (3 tbsp) raspberry jam over the base. Cream 50 g (2 oz) butter and 50 g (2 oz) caster sugar until light and fluffy and beat in the grated zest of 1 lemon with 1 large beaten egg. Fold in 75 g (3 oz) ground almonds with 75 g (3 oz) fine cake crumbs and mix with 15 ml (1 tbsp) milk or lemon juice to a soft dropping consistency. Spread smoothly over the jam.

Combination microwave Preheat the oven if necessary according to the manufacturer's instructions. Place on the wire rack or trivet for cooking.

Quantity	Temperature	Microwave Setting	Minutes
1 recipe above	250°C	Medium (50%)	13–15

Convection microwave Preheat the oven for 10 minutes or according to the manufacturer's instructions. Place on the wire rack or trivet for cooking. **Cook by convection first then by microwave.**

Quantity	Convection Temperature/Minutes	Microwave Setting/Time
1 recipe above	200°C/25 minutes	Medium (50%)/4 minutes

Microwave only Not suitable since the pastry and filling do not brown and crisp adequately.

BISCUITS

Basic Refrigerator Biscuits

This is a basic plain biscuit that can be prepared well in advance, flavoured as liked, and sliced and cooked according to daily requirements. The recipe will make about 50–60 biscuits. Sift 225 g (8 oz) plain flour with 5 ml (1 tsp) baking powder. Rub in 100 g (4 oz) butter. Mix in 175 g (6 oz) caster sugar and 1 beaten egg to make a firm dough. Roll into a long sausage shape, about 5 cm (2 in) in diameter and wrap in foil or cling film to store.

Combination microwave **Cook by convection only.** Cook only about 12 biscuits at a time. Preheat the oven according to the manufacturer's instructions. Place on a baking tray or heatproof plate to cook, well apart to allow for spreading. Leave to firm up for 3–4 minutes before transferring to a wire rack to cool.

Quantity	Convection Temperature	Minutes
12 biscuits maximum	180°C	10–15

***Convection microwave* Cook by convection only.** Cook only about 12 biscuits at a time. Preheat the oven for 10 minutes or according to the manufacturer's instructions. Place on a baking tray, well apart to allow for spreading. Leave to firm up for 3–4 minutes before transferring to a wire rack to cool.

Quantity	Convection Temperature	Minutes
12 biscuits maximum	180°C	10–15

Microwave only Biscuits can be cooked in the microwave only oven but do tend to have a very pale and soft appearance – ideally cook conventionally unless using dark coloured mixtures. Cook 6 at a time on a heatproof plate or special microwave baking tray. Leave until firm enough to handle before transferring to a wire rack to cool further.

Quantity	Microwave Setting	Minutes
6 biscuits	High (100%)	1½–1¾

Variations

Chocolate Refrigerator Biscuits Add 50 g (2 oz) finely-grated chocolate with the sugar to the above recipe.
Coconut Refrigerator Biscuits Add 50 g (2 oz) desiccated coconut with the sugar to the above recipe.
Currant or Raisin Refrigerator Biscuits Add 50 g (2 oz) chopped raisins or currants with the sugar to the above recipe.
Ginger Refrigerator Biscuits Sift 7.5 ml (1½ tsp) ground ginger with the flour in the above recipe.
Nutty Refrigerator Biscuits Add 50 g (2 oz) finely chopped nuts with the sugar to the above recipe.
Orange or Lemon Refrigerator Biscuits Add 2 teaspoons finely grated lemon rind or orange rind with the sugar to the above recipe.

MERINGUES

Whisk 2 egg whites until stiff then whisk in 50 g (2 oz) caster sugar until stiff and glossy. Fold in a further 50 g (2 oz) caster sugar with a metal spoon. Pipe or spoon small meringues on to greaseproof or rice paper.

Combination microwave **Cook by convection only.** Preheat the oven according to the manufacturer's instructions. Leave to dry in the oven.

Quantity	Convection Temperature	Minutes
1 recipe above	140°C	60–70

Convection microwave **Cook by convection only.** Preheat the oven according to the manufacturer's instructions. Leave to dry in the oven.

Quantity	Convection Temperature	Minutes
1 recipe above	130°C	70–80

Microwave only Traditional meringues cannot be cooked in the basic microwave oven. Special fondant icing mixtures can however be cooked to make sweet crisp meringue-like discs (see specialist recipe books).

PAVLOVA

Prepare a basic pavlova recipe by whisking 3 egg whites until stiff. Whisk in 75 g (3 oz) icing sugar until glossy. Whisk in 10 ml (2 tsp) vinegar. Sift a further 75 g (3 oz) icing sugar with 10 ml (2 tsp) cornflour and fold into the whisked mixture. spoon into a 23 cm (9 in) round on a foil lined baking sheet and lightly hollow the centre.

Combination microwave **Cook by convection only.** Preheat the oven if necessary according to the manufacturer's instructions. Cook until the pavlova is firm and set.

Quantity	Convection Temperature	Hours
1 recipe above	140°C	1½–2

Convection microwave **Cook by convection only.** Preheat the oven for 10 minutes or according to the manufacturer's instructions. Cook until the pavlova is firm and set.

Quantity	Convection Temperature	Hours
1 recipe above	130°C	1½–2

Microwave only Not suitable because the pavlova does not crisp and dry adequately.

SCONES

Plain and Fruited

Sift 225 g (8 oz) plain flour with 15 ml (1 tbsp) baking powder and a pinch of salt. Rub in 50 g (2 oz) butter until the mixture resembles fine breadcrumbs. Stir in 15 ml (1 tbsp) caster sugar and bind to a soft dough with about 150 ml (¼ pt) milk. If liked add 75 g (3 oz) sultanas with the sugar. Roll out on a lightly floured surface to about 4 cm (1½ in) thick and cut out 8–10 rounds using a 5 cm (2 in) cutter.

Combination microwave Cook by convection only. Preheat the oven if necessary according to the manufacturer's instructions. Place on a greased ovenproof tray or plate or on the turntable and allow to cool slightly before removing to a wire rack to cool.

Quantity	Convection Temperature	Minutes
8–10	220°C	12

Convection microwave Cook by convection only. Preheat the oven if necessary for 10 minutes or according to the manufacturer's instructions. Place on a baking tray on the convection rack or trivet to cook. Allow to cool slightly before removing to a wire rack to cool.

Quantity	Convection Temperature	Minutes
8–10	220°C	12

Microwave only Preheat a large browning dish according to the manufacturer's instructions. Lightly brush the base with oil. Add the scones, pressing down well and cook for 1 minute of the cooking time. Turn over and cook for the remaining time. Transfer to a wire rack to cool.

Quantity	Microwave Setting	Minutes
8–10	High (100%)	2–2½

SHORTBREAD

Cream 100 g (4 oz) butter with 50 g (2 oz) caster sugar. Add 150 g (5 oz) plain flour and 25 g (1 oz) semolina or rice flour and mix well. Press into a greased 18-20 cm (7–8 in) round flan dish and prick thoroughly with a fork.

Combination microwave Preheat the oven, if necessary, according to the manufacturer's instructions. Allow to cool in the dish before marking into wedges with a knife and sprinkling with extra caster sugar. When firm allow to cool on a wire rack.

Quantity	Temperature	Microwave Setting	Minutes
1 recipe above	180°C	Low (30%)	11

Convection microwave Preheat the oven for 10 minutes or according to the manufacturer's instructions. **Cook by convection only.** Allow to cool in the dish before marking into wedges with a knife and sprinkling with extra caster sugar. When firm allow to cool on a wire rack.

Quantity	Convection Temperature	Minutes
1 recipe above	150°C	30

Microwave only Allow to cool in the dish before marking into wedges with a knife and sprinkling with extra caster sugar. When firm to the touch allow to cool on a wire rack.

Quantity	Microwave Setting	Minutes
1 recipe above	High (100%)	2½–3½

SAVOURIES

CORNISH PASTIES

Mix 225 g (8 oz) minced or shredded beef with 2 small chopped potatoes, 1 chopped onion, 2.5 ml (½ tsp) dried mixed herbs, 15 ml (1 tbsp) chopped parsley, 30 ml (2 tbsp) beef stock and salt and pepper to taste. Roll out 225 g (8 oz) shortcrust pastry, ie, pastry made with 225 g (8 oz) plain flour, 100 g (4 oz) butter and 60 ml (4 tbsp) iced water, and cut out 4 × 20 cm (8 in) circles. Divide the filling between the rounds and draw the rounds up to make pasties with a seam across the top. Crimp the seams attractively and glaze with beaten egg. Place on an ovenproof plate or tray to cook.

Combination microwave Preheat the oven if necessary according to the manufacturer's instructions.

Quantity	Temperature	Microwave Setting	Minutes
4	220°C	Medium (50%)	17–18½

Convection microwave Preheat the oven for 10 minutes or according to the manufacturer's instructions. **Cook by convection first then by microwave.**

Quantity	Convection Temperature/Minutes	Microwave Setting/Minutes
4	230°C/10 minutes then 160°C/30 minutes	Medium (50%)/4 minutes

Microwave only Not suitable since the pastry does not crisp and brown adequately.

ECLAIRS
Sweet and Savoury

Prepare a basic choux pastry mixture: place 150 ml (¼ pt) water and 50 g (2 oz) butter in a bowl and **cook on microwave only** High (100%) power for 2 minutes until the mixture boils. Add 65 g (2½ oz) plain flour and **cook on microwave only** High (100%) power for 1 minute. Gradually beat in 2 eggs until the mixture is thick and glossy. Then fill a piping bag with a large plain nozzle and pipe 7.5 cm (3 in) lengths of the mixture well apart on a baking tray or the greased turntable of the oven. After cooking fill with either a sweet or savoury mixture.

Combination and convection microwave Cook by convection only. Preheat the oven if necessary according to the manufacturer's instructions. After cooking make a small slit in the side of each eclair to allow the steam to escape. Allow to cool on a wire rack.

Quantity	Convection Temperature	Minutes
1 quantity above (to make about 12)	200°C	25

Microwave only Not suitable since the pastry does not brown and crisp.

FLANS AND QUICHES
Cooking Shortcrust Pastry Flan Case

Roll out 175 g (6 oz) shortcrust pastry on a lightly floured surface to a round large enough to line a 20 cm (8 in) flan dish. Press in firmly taking care not to stretch the pastry and trim away carefully. If time allows then leave to 'rest' in the refrigerator for 15 minutes. Prick the base and sides well.

Combination microwave Line the flan with greaseproof paper and baking beans. Preheat the oven if necessary according to the manufacturer's instructions. Remove the greaseproof paper and beans for the last 5 minutes cooking time.

Quantity	Temperature	Microwave Setting	Minutes
1 recipe above	200°C	Medium (50%)	9–14

Convection microwave Either cook the flan case **by convection only** or **by microwave only** (see instructions below). Preheat the oven for 10 minutes or according to the manufacturer's instructions. Line the flan case with greaseproof paper and baking beans. Remove the greaseproof paper and beans for the last 5 minutes cooking time.

Quantity	Convection Temperature	Minutes
1 recipe above	200°C	15–18

Microwave only Place a double thickness layer of absorbent kitchen towel in the base of the flan, easing it into position around the edges. Remove the paper after 3½ minutes cooking time.

Quantity	Microwave Setting	Minutes
1 recipe above	High (100%)	4

Adding Uncooked Filling to a Flan Case

Allow any pre-cooked pastry case to cool slightly before adding the uncooked filling mixture. Timings for cooking the fillings will vary depending upon the type and quantity of filling but the following are good guidelines:

Combination microwave If necessary lower the convection setting (after cooking the flan case).

Quantity	Temperature	Microwave Setting	Minutes
20 cm (8 in) filled flan	180°	Low (30%)	14–18½

NOTE: If the flan case has not been pre-cooked and the filling is added to the uncooked flan case the following times apply (remember to preheat the oven according to the manufacturer's instructions):

Quantity	Temperature	Microwave Setting	Minutes
20 cm (8 in) filled flan	200°	Low (30%)	18½–21

Convection microwave Either cook **by convection** or **by microwave only** (see instructions below).

Quantity	Convection Temperature	Minutes
20 cm (8 in) filled flan	200°C	25

Microwave only Allow the cooked flan to stand, covered, for 10–15 minutes to finish cooking. When cooked the centre of the flan will still appear a little wet and wobbly but will firm during the standing time.

Quantity	Microwave Setting	Minutes
20 cm (8 in) filled flan	Low (30%)	13–15

SAUSAGE ROLLS

Prepare (or use 10–20 ready-made) regular-size (not cocktail) sausage rolls. Glaze with beaten egg before cooking.

Combination microwave Preheat the oven if necessary according to the manufacturer's instructions. Most combination ovens will cook up to 12 regular-size sausage rolls comfortably in one operation. Place on ovenproof plates or trays and position one on the base or turntable of the oven and one on the wire rack above. Cook as below removing the batch on the wire rack after 10 minutes cooking time (when cooked and golden) and transferring the second batch from the base of the oven to the wire rack for the remainder of the cooking time.

Quantity	Temperature	Microwave Setting	Minutes
12	250°C	Medium (50%)	11–12

Convection microwave Preheat the oven for 10 minutes or according to the manufacturer's instructions. Place on ovenproof plates or trays and place on the turntable or base and baking trivet, changing the trays over after half of the cooking time.

Quantity	Convection Temperature	Minutes
12	220°C	25–30

Microwave only Not suitable for cooking since the pastry does not brown and crisp adequately. The microwave will however reheat cooked sausage rolls for serving. Leave to stand for 3 minutes before serving.

Quantity	Microwave Setting	Minutes
6	High (100%)	1½–2½

TOAD IN THE HOLE

Place 450 g (1 lb) skinless pork sausages in a lightly greased large baking dish or 25 cm (10 in) flan dish. Make the batter by sifting 100 g (4 oz) plain flour with a pinch of salt into a bowl. Make a well in the centre and crack in 2 eggs. Gradually beat the eggs into the flour with 300 ml (½ pt) milk and mix to a smooth batter.

Combination microwave Preheat the oven if necessary according to the manufacturer's instructions. Pour the batter over the sausages and cook as below until well-risen, crisp and golden.

Quantity	Temperature	Microwave Setting	Minutes
1 recipe above	240°C	Medium (50%)	17–18½

Convection microwave **Cook by convection only.** Preheat the oven for 10 minutes or according to the manufacturer's instructions. Cook the sausages alone for 10 minutes then pour over the batter. Return to the oven and cook for the time below.

Quantity	Convection Temperature	Minutes
1 recipe above	230°C	25–30

Microwave only Not suitable since the batter does not brown and crisp adequately.

YORKSHIRE PUDDING

Make the batter by sifting 100 g (4 oz) plain flour with a pinch of salt into a bowl. Make a well in the centre and crack in 2 eggs. Gradually beat the eggs into the flour with 300 ml (½ pt) milk and mix to a smooth batter. Spoon into a well greased large pie plate, ovenproof dish or tin (if metal allowed) or into 6 ramekin dishes.

Combination microwave Preheat the oven for 10 minutes or according to the manufacturer's instructions.

Quantity	Temperature	Microwave Setting	Minutes
1 large as above	250°C	High (100%)	16
6 small as above	250°C	Medium (50%)	15

Convection microwave **Cook by convection only.** Preheat the oven for 10 minutes or according to the manufacturer's instructions.

Quantity	Convection Temperature	Minutes
1 large as above	210°C	30–40
6 small as above	220°C	20–25

Microwave only Not suitable since the batter does not brown and crisp adequately.

DRINKS

COCOA AND DRINKING CHOCOLATE

Place 2 heaped teaspoons (about 12 ml) cocoa or drinking chocolate in a large jug. Add sugar to taste if making cocoa (about 15 ml [1 tbsp]). Blend in 150 ml (¼ pt) milk.

Combination microwave **Cook by microwave only.** Cook the cocoa or drinking chocolate mixture on High (100%) for 1–1½ minutes. Add a further 300 ml (½ pt) milk and cook as below, whisking twice. Pour into warm mugs to serve.

Quantity	Microwave Setting	Minutes
1 recipe above, to serve 2	High (100%)	1–2

Convection microwave and microwave only **Cook by microwave only.** Cook the cocoa or drinking chocolate mixture on High (100%) for 1–1½ minutes. Add a further 300 ml (½ pt) milk and cook as below, whisking twice. Pour into warm mugs to serve.

Quantity	Microwave Setting	Minutes
1 recipe above, to serve 2	High (100%)	¾–1½

COFFEE

A Cup of Instant Coffee

Place 5 ml (1 tsp) of instant coffee in a mug with 150 ml (¼ pt) water.

***Combination microwave, convection microwave and microwave only.* Cook by microwave only.** Heat as below until steaming then add milk and sugar if liked.

Quantity	Microwave Setting	Minutes
1 mug	High (100%)	1¼–2

To Reheat Prepared Fresh Black Coffee

Times here refer to reheating cold filtered or percolated coffee.

***Combination microwave* Cook by microwave only.** Place in a large jug and cook as below.

Quantity	Microwave Setting	Minutes
600 ml (1 pt)	High (100%)	4–5
1.2 litres (2 pt)	High (100%)	7–8

***Convection microwave and microwave only* Cook by microwave only.** Place in a large jug and cook as below.

Quantity	Microwave Setting	Minutes
600 ml (1 pt)	High (100%)	3¾–4
1.2 litres (2 pt)	High (100%)	6½–6¾

To Heat Prepared Fresh Black Coffee and Milk Together

Times here refer to reheating cold filtered or percolated coffee and chilled milk in separate jugs for serving together.

***Combination microwave* Cook by microwave only.** Place the coffee and milk in separate jugs and cook as below.

Quantity	Microwave Setting	Minutes
600 ml (1 pt) coffee with 150 ml (¼ pt) milk	High (100%)	5–6
1.2 litres (2 pt) coffee with 300 ml (½ pt) milk	High (100%)	8–9

Convection microwave and microwave only **Cook by microwave only.** Place the coffee and milk in separate jugs for serving together.

Quantity	Microwave Setting	Minutes
600 ml (1 pt) coffee with 150 ml (¼ pt) milk	High (100%)	4–4½
1.2 litres (2 pt) coffee with 300 ml (½ pt) milk	High (100%)	7–7½

Liqueur Coffee

Divide 60 ml (4 tbsp) chosen liqueur between 2 heatproof glasses. Add 30 ml (2 tbsp) of sugar and 150 ml (¼ pt) cold or hot coffee to each glass.

Combination microwave **Cook by microwave only.** Cook for the shorter time if hot coffee has been used and the longer if cold coffee is used. Stir well at the end of the cooking time and float cream on top to serve.

Quantity	Microwave Setting	Minutes
1 recipe above, to serve 2	High (100%)	1½–2½

Convection microwave and microwave only **Cook by microwave only.** Cook for the shorter time if hot coffee has been used and the longer if cold coffee is used. Stir well at the end of the cooking time and float cream on top to serve.

Quantity	Microwave Setting	Minutes
1 recipe above, to serve 2	High (100%)	1½–2½

Milk

Hot Milk

Place in a large jug since mixture rises upon heating.

Combination microwave Cook by microwave only. Pour into mugs to serve or use as required in cooking, baking or to serve with coffee.

Quantity	Microwave Setting	Minutes
150 ml (¼ pt)	High (100%)	1¼–1¾
300 ml (½ pt)	High (100%)	2–2½

Convection microwave Cook by microwave only. Pour into mugs to serve or use as required in cooking, baking or to serve with coffee.

Quantity	Microwave Setting	Minutes
150 ml (¼ pt)	High (100%)	¾–1¼
300 ml (½ pt)	High (100%)	1½–2

TEA

To Brew Fresh Tea

Place 750 ml (1¼ pt) water in a large jug.

Combination microwave Cook by microwave only. Cook as below until the water is boiling then add 20 ml (4 tsp) loose tea or 3 tea bags and stir well. Cover and leave to infuse until strength is as liked.

Quantity	Microwave Setting	Minutes
1 recipe as above, to serve 4	High (100%)	5–6½

Convection microwave and microwave only Cook by microwave only. Cook as below until the water is boiling then add 20 ml (4 tsp) loose tea or 3 tea bags and stir well. Cover and leave to infuse until strength is as liked.

Quantity	Microwave Setting	Minutes
1 recipe as above, to serve 4	High (100%)	4–5

ESSENTIAL FOODS AND INGREDIENTS

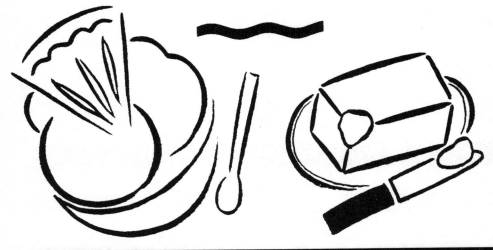

BREADCRUMBS

To Dry Bread for Crumbs

Place the bread slice on a plate and cook until dry, but do check regularly to prevent scorching. Leave to dry and harden before crumbling or grating to make dry crumbs.

Combination microwave Cook by microwave only.

Quantity	Microwave Setting	Minutes
1 slice of bread	High (100%)	2–3

Convection microwave and microwave only Cook by microwave only.

Quantity	Microwave Setting	Minutes
1 slice of bread	High (100%)	1½–2½

BUTTER

To Soften Chilled for Spreading

Place the chilled butter in a serving dish and microwave, checking constantly to make sure the butter does not melt.

Combination microwave **Cook by microwave only.**

Quantity	Microwave Setting	Minutes
100 g (4 oz)	Medium (50%)	½–¾
250 g (9 oz) block	Medium (50%)	1

Convection microwave and microwave only **Cook by microwave only.**

Quantity	Microwave Setting	Minutes
100 g (4 oz)	Medium (50%)	¼–½
250 g (9 oz) block	Medium (50%)	¾

To Melt Butter

Place the butter in a dish, cover to reduce spattering.

Combination microwave **Cook by microwave only.**

Quantity	Microwave Setting	Minutes
25 g (1 oz)	High (100%)	¼–½
50 g (2 oz)	High (100%)	1
100 g (4 oz)	High (100%)	1¼–1½

Convection microwave and microwave only **Cook by microwave only.**

Quantity	Microwave Setting	Minutes
25 g (1 oz)	High (100%)	¼–½
50 g (2 oz)	High (100%)	¾
100 g (4 oz)	High (100%)	1–1¼

CARAMEL

To Cook Caramel

Place 50 g (2 oz) sugar and 30 ml (2 tbsp) water in a small heatproof bowl.

Combination microwave **Cook by microwave only.** Stir every 1 minute until golden then pour into a mould (if using to make crème caramel) or on to an oiled tray for making pieces of crushed caramel and leave to set. Leave until cold before handling.

Quantity	Microwave Setting	Minutes
1 recipe above	High (100%)	3½–4

Convection microwave and microwave only **Cook by microwave only.** Stir every 1 minute until golden then pour into a mould (if using to make crème caramel) or on to an oiled tray for making pieces of crushed caramel and leave to set. Leave until cold before handling.

Quantity	Microwave Setting	Minutes
1 recipe above	High (100%)	3–3½

CHOCOLATE

To Melt Chocolate

Break the chocolate into small pieces and place in a cooking dish. Check often during cooking to prevent scorching.

Combination microwave **Cook by microwave only.** Stir twice during the cooking time.

Quantity	Microwave Setting	Minutes
50 g (2 oz) plain dessert	Medium (50%)	2–2½
50 g (2 oz) milk dessert	Medium (50%)	1½–2½
50 g (2 oz) white	Medium (50%)	1¼–1¾
50 g (2 oz) cooking	Medium (50%)	3–3½
50 g (2 oz) chocolate chips	Medium (50%)	2¼–3½
100 g (4 oz) plain dessert	Medium (50%)	2½–3
100 g (4 oz) milk dessert	Medium (50%)	2½–3¼
100 g (4 oz) white	Medium (50%)	1½–2½
100 g (4 oz) cooking	Medium (50%)	3¾–4
100 g (4 oz) chocolate chips	Medium (50%)	3½–4

Convection microwave and microwave only **Cook by microwave only.** Stir twice during the cooking time.

Quantity	Microwave Setting	Minutes
50 g (2 oz) plain dessert	Medium (50%)	1½–2
50 g (2 oz) milk dessert	Medium (50%)	1½–2¼
50 g (2 oz) white	Medium (50%)	1–1½
50 g (2 oz) cooking	Medium (50%)	2½–3
50 g (2 oz) chocolate chips	Medium (50%)	2–3
100 g (4 oz) plain dessert	Medium (50%)	2–3
100 g (4 oz) milk dessert	Medium (50%)	2–2¾
100 g (4 oz) white	Medium (50%)	1¼–2
100 g (4 oz) cooking	Medium (50%)	3½–3¾
100 g (4 oz) chocolate chips	Medium (50%)	3–3¾

COCONUT

To Toast Desiccated Coconut

Place the coconut on a large heatproof plate. Stir every 1 minute of the cooking time until golden. Cool before storing to use.

Combination microwave **Cook by microwave only.**

Quantity	Microwave Setting	Minutes
100 g (4 oz)	High (100%)	5–6

Convection microwave and microwave only **Cook by microwave only.**

Quantity	Microwave Setting	Minutes
100 g (4 oz)	High (100%)	4–5

FROZEN PASTRY

To Defrost Frozen Ready-prepared Shortcrust and Puff Pastry

Leave in the plastic wrapping if shop bought or place on a plate and cover with microwave cling film. Check frequently to prevent hot spots.

Combination microwave **Cook by microwave only.** Turn over to rearrange once during the cooking time. Leave to stand for 5 minutes before using.

Quantity	Microwave Setting	Minutes
210 g (7½ oz) pkt	Defrost (20%)	2½–3
370 g (13 oz) pkt	Defrost (20%)	3½–4¼

Convection microwave and microwave only Cook **by microwave only.** Turn over or rearrange once during the cooking time. Leave to stand for 5 minutes before using.

Quantity	Microwave Setting	Minutes
210 g (7½ oz) pkt	Defrost (20%)	2–3
370 g (13 oz) pkt	Defrost (20%)	3½

GELATINE

Dissolving Powdered Gelatine

Place the liquid in a small cup or bowl and sprinkle over the powdered gelatine. Leave until spongy – about 5 minutes. Cook as below until clear and dissolved.

Combination microwave, convection microwave and microwave only Cook **by microwave only.**

Quantity	Microwave Setting	Minutes
up to 150 ml (¼ pt)	High (100%)	¼–1

HONEY

To Clear Crystallised Honey

Remove any metal cap from the jar of honey.

Combination microwave Cook **by microwave only.** Stir once, halfway through the cooking time. Reduce the cooking time for part-filled jars accordingly.

Quantity	Microwave Setting	Minutes
450 g (1 lb) jar	High (100%)	1½–2

Convection microwave and microwave only Cook **by microwave only.** Stir once, halfway through the cooking time. Reduce the cooking time for part-filled jars accordingly.

Quantity	Microwave Setting	Minutes
450 g (1 lb) jar	High (100%)	1¼–1½

ICE CREAM, SORBET AND WATER ICES
To Soften for Scooping

Only for hard, not soft-scoop varieties of the above. Remove any metal or foil lids if necessary.

Combination microwave **Cook by microwave only.** Leave in the container and check constantly. Leave to stand for 1 minute before scooping to serve.

Quantity	Microwave Setting	Minutes
about 1 litre (1¾ pt)	Medium (50%)	½–1¼

Convection microwave and microwave only **Cook by microwave only.** Leave in the container and check constantly. Leave to stand for 1 minute before scooping to serve.

Quantity	Microwave Setting	Minutes
about 1 litre (1¾ pt)	Medium (50%)	¼–1¼

STOCKS
Meat, Chicken, Vegetable and Fish Stock

Place meat bones, poultry carcass, selection of flavouring vegetables or fish head, tail and trimmings in a bowl with a bouquet garni and seasoning to taste. Cover with boiling water.

Combination microwave, convection microwave and microwave only **Cook by microwave only.** Cover to cook and stir twice during the cooking time. Top up with water to cover the ingredients if necessary during cooking. Strain and cool completely before using. Store vegetable stock in the refrigerator for up to 48 hours (or 6 months in freezer); poultry stock for up to 48 hours (or 6 months in freezer); vegetable stock for up to 24 hours (or 3 months in freezer); and fish stock for up to 24 hours (do not freeze).

Stock Type	Microwave Setting	Minutes
Fish stock	High (100%)	9–11
Meat stock	High (100%)	37–45
Poultry stock	High (100%)	18–23
Vegetable stock	High (100%)	14–18

SUGAR SYRUP

Sugar Syrup for Poaching Fruits and Short-term Bottling

Place 300 ml (½ pt) water and 100 g (4 oz) sugar in a large heatproof jug with a few flavourings if liked (eg citrus peel, cinnamon stick, whole cloves etc).

Combination microwave **Cook by microwave only.** Stir three times during cooking.

Quantity	Microwave Setting	Minutes
Makes 300 ml (½ pt)	High (100%)	4–5

Convection microwave and microwave only **Cook by microwave only.** Stir three times during cooking.

Quantity	Microwave Setting	Minutes
Makes 300 ml (½ pt)	High (100%)	3½–4

YEAST AND BREAD DOUGHS

Hastening Proving of Yeast and Bread Doughs

Place the prepared dough in a bowl and cover.

Combination microwave, convection microwave and microwave only Give the dough short bursts of microwave energy as below, observing a 10 minute standing time between each, until the dough has risen to double its size.

Quantity	Microwave Setting	Seconds
about 900 g (2 lb) piece of dough	High (100%)	5–10

MICROWAVE ROUND-UP

The basics and skills of conventional cooking have usually been learnt over a period of years at our mother's knee, at school, by trial and error, through cookery books and cookery courses, or simply by watching others. These skills and basics enable us to know not only how to cook food but to know when it is cooked; to time the cooking of one dish alongside the cooking of another so that they are ready simultaneously; to prepare separate courses for a meal with ease for serving; and in general to prepare a wide variety of dishes for meals as diverse as breakfast and supper with few failures.

Many of these basics have had to be rethought or relearnt with the microwave oven and its special new and often unfamiliar cooking action. So too have the skills of general family food preparation and meal planning where the microwave is the main cooking appliance. This book with its introductory classes for all types of microwave, its at-a-glance instructions for cooking foods as basic but as different as chocolate and cheese; and its recipes for mainstay family fare will arm you with many of the basic skills for successful microwave cooking.

Despite this there will still be some microwave cooks who will flounder and not get the best from their machine (I say that with some experience, since I didn't really start to get to grips with my first microwave for a good many months). The reasons for this are not hard to understand – it is easy to slip back to familiar and safe cooking methods, even if they are not so convenient; to use the microwave just as a back-up to the conventional oven or hob; to find it is ideal for cooking one dish, but what about cooking more than one?; and in general to decide that the microwave isn't all it is cracked up to be.

If you are one of the latter type I hope this final section will convince you to soldier on – it really is worth it. Try to think microwave, forget about too many specifics and follow (and dare I say learn) some new basic general guidelines, then be bold. What follows are my general guidelines, based on years of cooking in the microwave, for everyday cooking, condensed into a few pages. I hope they tip the balance in your favour or will bridge the gap between your being a half-hearted microwave cook and a microwave devotee or enthusiast.

BASIC MICROWAVE SUCCESS

Fish and Shellfish

Most fish and shellfish dishes require a moist cooking method so the microwave only mode is the best choice here. However, if some degree of browning is required or even a little crisping then consider cooking by combination or convection. Convection only is definitely the best choice for fish in batter or fish in breadcrumbs although some success can be achieved with combination cooking.

If cooking by microwave only then follow the specific individual instructions relating to that food. If combination baking then also check the specific instructions or follow the general guidelines of:

COMBINATION COOKING at 180–200°C on **LOW** (30%) power

Meat and Poultry

When roasting meat and poultry opt for the combination mode whether in the combination oven or convection oven. Manufacturers differ enormously when giving instructions for roasting meat. Some choose to go for a high temperature and low microwave setting, others for a medium temperature and high microwave setting. I have found that the lower microwave setting with a fairly high temperature, although taking longer, gives tastier, more succulent and more evenly cooked, traditional-style results. There seems to be less shrinkage of roasts and even less tender cuts cook well. No very special techniques need to be observed; simply prepare in the normal way, but try to achieve a compact shape for cooking. Turn the meat a little more frequently than you would conventionally and do ensure that you observe the standing times at the end of cooking – this will help to finish cooking the meat and make it easier for carving. If you have a rather fatty piece of meat then you may like to consider cooking in a roasting bag for all or part of the time to reduce spattering on the oven walls. Keep any collected juices from roasting meats to make a gravy for serving with the joint.

Smaller cuts of meat can also be combination cooked with success but if the cooking times are very short then browning may not be as good as conventional cooking. Convection cooking probably gives better browning but will take a little longer than combination cooking. If your combination microwave has a grill then cook by combination/grilling, following either the instructions in this book or your combination microwave manufacturer's handbook.

Stews, pot roasts and casseroles can be cooked either by combination or microwave alone. If you have a favourite family-size casserole recipe and are unsure about cooking temperatures, microwave settings and time then follow the general guidelines of:

COMBINATION COOKING at 160°C on **LOW** (30%)
for about 45–55 minutes

Pot roasts can be cooked by microwave or combination and timings will depend upon the tenderness and quality of the meat. The following guidelines have been found to give good general results:

GOOD QUALITY at 180–200°C on **LOW** (30%) for
18–23 minutes per 450 g (1 lb)
CHEAP CUTS at 150–160°C on **LOW** (30%) for
32-40 minutes per 450 g (1 lb)

Vegetables

Boiled and steamed vegetables are still best cooked on the microwave only mode. They cook crisp/tender, are colourful and full of nutritional value. Should you wish to bake vegetables (eg peppers) where some degree of browning and crisping is required then cook by combination or convection only. For made-up dishes the best general advice is:

COMBINATION COOK at 180–200°C on **LOW** (30%) power for 9–14 minutes
(then start checking until the food is cooked to your liking)

Jacket potatoes can be cooked in a number of ways, either combination baked at a high temperature with medium power setting or faster still on a high temperature with high power setting. The choice is yours, depending really upon how crisp you like your potatoes. The longer cooking time on microwave medium power will give crisper results.

Roast potatoes and parsnips can be cooked with any roast, placed under the joint to roast in the meat drippings, usually for about the last 20–30 minutes cooking time.

137

Pasta and Rice

Plain cooked rice and pasta should be cooked by microwave only. There won't be any time advantage to cooking these foods in the microwave over conventional methods but you will get al dente or fluffy separate results with little fear of sticky pans to scour! However if you are planning to serve with other foods you may like to cook them conventionally, leaving your microwave free to cook the accompaniments.

Baked pasta dishes, however, cook very well in the combination mode and by convection only — giving tender, golden and crisp baked results. Ideally, for a family-size dish:

COMBINATION COOKING at 200°C on **MEDIUM** (50%) power
for 18–22 minutes

Eggs and Cheese

Most egg and cheese dishes are best cooked by microwave only. Certainly the basic egg dishes that are poached, scrambled and steam baked. The exception is a baked soufflé. Microwave enthusiasts in the past have been able to get a soufflé to cook in the microwave only oven but it was a sorry sight with its pale appearance (I have a friend who described one of my efforts as looking like a swollen cork!). The introduction of convected heat to the microwave gives this classic dish a new lease of life. I found the best results were obtained by cooking a family size soufflé in the convection only oven:

CONVECTION ONLY at 200°C for about 25 minutes

However you can't beat the speed of the combination oven even if the result is a little inferior:

COMBINATION COOK at 250°C on **HIGH** (100%) for 6½–7 minutes

Breads

Home breadmaking should make a comeback with the combination microwave oven. Yeast mixtures can be quickly made, hastily proved then cooked either by combination or by convection only in a fraction of the time it takes conventionally. Individual recipes should always be followed for excellent results but when in doubt follow these basic guidelines:

COMBINATION COOK at 200°C on **LOW** (30%) or **MEDIUM** (50%) power
for 11–23 minutes (depending upon size of loaf)

Cakes

Large cakes that usually take a long time to cook conventionally are best cooked by combination microwave for good results. These include fruit cakes, Madeira cakes, gingerbreads, moist tea loaves etc. Layer sponges, small fairy and queen cakes, meringues and small biscuits are better cooked by convection only where they will brown and crisp more readily. Always take advice from your manufacturer's handbook here about the question of preheating. Most of the recipes I have tried in a multitude of ovens do benefit from a degree of preheating. It is difficult to give hard and fast rules here to follow since cake mixtures vary so much in composition but here goes:

COMBINATION COOK at 160–200°C on **LOW** (30%) power

Opt for the lower temperature if the cake usually takes a long time to cook (like a rich fruit cake) and the higher for a lighter tea loaf.
For convection only baking of breads, cakes and scones then cook:

CONVECTION ONLY at 10°C **LOWER** than conventionally
and shorten the cooking time

Pastries

Large pastry pies, quiches, flans and tarts cook very well on the combination mode – their generally longer cooking times affording a good degree of browning and crisping alongside tender cooking. Smaller pies, individual tarts and small crisp pastry items are often better cooked by convection only.

In the case of flans and quiches some manufacturers say that pre-cooking or baking 'blind' is unnecessary – take your manufacturer's advice. In 9 out of 10 of the ovens I have cooked on I prefer to pre-cook in the combination or convection only oven (I hate soggy and raw quiche bases). See the individual instructions on page 143.

Large meat and poultry pies can be cooked with great success whether you pre-cook the filling or not. Pre-cooking the filling probably gives safer, surer results and in general:

COMBINATION COOK at 200°C on **LOW** (30%) or **MEDIUM** (50%) – depending upon pie type

A large double-crust pie will usually take about 22–32 minutes and a single-crust about 18-27 minutes. Better browning and crisping is usually achieved with the lower power setting and longer time but should you opt to cook faster on Medium (50%) power and want to give a browning and crisping boost at the end of cooking, simply turn up the convection only controls for a few minutes and cook by convection only.

CHOOSING THE BEST COOKING MODE

The chart below is a guide to help you choose the best cooking mode, and get the best of all worlds, for a wide selection of basic everyday foods and dishes. It assumes, of course, that you have more than one cooking mode on offer. Basic microwave oven owners will only have microwave only to cook on – if this isn't the recommended method then turn to the relevant section in the book and take advice. Microwave only cooking may be just as acceptable or not at all suitable in which case you may be better cooking this food or dish conventionally.

Basic Food	Combination	Comb Convection	Convection only	Microwave only
FISH AND SHELLFISH				
Poached Fish				x
Baked Fish	x			
Fish Cakes	x		x	
Fish Fingers	x		x	
Fish Roes				x
Reheat Shellfish				x
Mussels				x
Fish in Pastry	x		x	
Raw Shellfish				x
Fish Soufflés			x	
Defrosting Fish				x
POULTRY AND GAME				
Chicken Portions	x	x		
Roast Whole Chicken	x	x		
Chicken Livers				x
Roast Duck	x	x		
Game Birds	x	x		
Poussins	x	x		
Roast Turkey	x	x		
Casseroles	x			x
Poultry and game pies, large	x			
Poultry and game pies, small			x	

Basic Food	Combination	Comb Convection	Convection only	Microwave only
MEAT				
Bacon			x	
Roast Beef	x	x		
Minced Beef				x
Gammon Steaks	x		x	
Hamburgers	x		x	
Kidneys	x			
Roast Lamb	x	x		
Lamb Chops	x		x	
Liver	x			
Meatloaf	x		x	
Pâté	x			
Roast Pork	x	x		
Pork Chops	x		x	
Sausages	x		x	
Steaks	x		x	
Roast Veal	x	x		
VEGETABLES				
Boiled or Steamed				x
Baked in Jacket	x			
Reheating Canned				x
Cooking Frozen				x
Roast Vegetables (eg potatoes)	x	x		
Stuffed, Baked Vegetables	x		x	
Vegetable Gratins	x	x		
Vegetable Crumbles	x			
PASTA AND RICE				
Boiled Pasta				x
Reheating Canned				x
Baked lasagnas	x	x		
Boiled Rice				x
EGGS AND CHEESE				
Baked Eggs				x
Poached Eggs				x
Scrambled Eggs				x
Soufflés	x		x	
Softening Cheese				x

Basic Food	Combination	Comb Convection	Convection only	Microwave only
GRAINS, NUTS AND PULSES				
Boiling grains				x
Toasting Nuts				x
Roasting Nuts			x	x
Cooking Dried Beans				x
Cooking Dried Peas				x
Cooking Lentils				x
SAUCES				
All Sauces				x
FRUIT AND BASIC PUDDINGS				
Poached Fruit				x
Stewed Fruit				x
Baked Fruit			x	x
Baked in Pastry	x			
Fruit Pies	x		x	
Sponge Pudding				x
Bread and Butter Pudding	x			
Christmas Pudding				x
Eve's Pudding	x	x		
Fruit Crumble	x	x		
Roly Poly	x	x		
BREAD, CAKES, PASTRIES AND BAKES				
Bread			x	
Cakes, large	x	x		
Cakes, small			x	
Pastries	x	x	x	
Quiches	x		x	
Biscuits			x	
Meringues			x	
Pavlova			x	
Scones			x	
Shortbread			x	
Yorkshire Pudding	x		x	

Basic Food	Combination	Comb Convection	Convection only	Microwave only
CONVENIENCE FOODS				
Canned beans				x
Pies and Pastries	x		x	
Plated Meals				x
Casseroles				x
Fish in Sauce				x
Gratins and Baked Ready Meals	x		x	
Pizza			x	
Part-Baked Bread	x		x	
Bread and Cake Mixes	x		x	
Potato Products	x		x	
Pastry Puddings	x		x	
Quiches			x	
BEVERAGES				
All types				x
OTHER BASICS				
General Defrosting				x
Preserves				x
Soups				x
Surface Browning and Cooking	x	x	x	

MEAL AND MENU PLANNING

It may seem difficult, yet is very easy to cook meals with many different dishes and whole 3 or 4 course menus efficiently in the microwave oven. It is easier still if you also use your conventional oven and hob alongside the microwave to get the very best of all worlds. Thousands of microwave cooks will tell you that it just takes, like many other things, patience and experience and will come easily in time. With a little thought and perhaps more careful planning than you are used to, complete meals and menus can be cooked right from the start. Just follow these guidelines and tips:

★ Start by trying one course of a simple main meal cooked in the microwave (with more than one dish). Serve with a cold starter and dessert. Cook the main dish first wherever possible and while this is standing cook the accompaniments. All the separate dishes will then be ready at the same time. For speed, make sure that any foods that have been frozen are thoroughly defrosted before cooking.

★ If roasting in the combination oven or convection oven where the oven will be hot then par-cook vegetables first then finish in the microwave later after cooking the roast. If you cook them after the roast when the oven is still hot they may dry out too much and have a parched look.

★ Crisp pastry items and baked batters like Yorkshire puddings should be cooked at the very last moment since they will quickly lose their crispness.

★ When you feel confident move on to a more adventurous menu and try cooking a hot pudding. At first try a short cooking one that can be cooked while you are seated eating the main course. For obvious reasons choose a recipe that does not need too much attention; a fruit crumble or pie for example. Prepare it ahead and simply pop into the oven after cooking the main course.

★ Worried about heating plates to serve with microwave cooked foods (since there isn't a warming drawer to your oven)? Simply pop in a bowl of warm water until needed. A quick wipe will leave them piping hot for receiving food. Alternatively consider buying a special electric plate warmer that looks a bit like a 'plate glove' for multiple plate warming.

★ When cooking a whole host of different dishes then line them up in order of cooking order until you are sure and familiar with their sequence.

★ It may be worth investing in a small warming tray if you regularly cook lots of different dishes in the microwave oven, although this isn't strictly necessary since the microwave will reheat food in minutes without over-cooking, drying out or having that reheated taste.

★ Remember to wipe up spills and spatters as they happen or while the oven is still warm (in the case of convection or combination ovens) rather than face them later when hard and baked-on.

BASIC-BASICS TOP TEN TIPS

By all means use whatever general cooking equipment you have for microwave cooking (after checking its suitability), but for good all-round use in all kinds of microwave, conventional oven, traditional hob and freezer buy ceramic or glass ovenware like Pyrex.

★ Don't be a slave to your microwave – use it only when it will save you time or give you good results. There are no prizes for eating poorly-cooked dishes just because they have been cooked in the microwave. Use your microwave as an adjunct to your conventional oven and hob.

★ In the early stages of cooking by microwave think carefully and check the best method of cooking – by combination, convection combination, convection only or by microwave only. The charts on pages 16–18 are a good starting point.

★ The microwave, regardless of type, isn't a set-it and forget-it machine. Follow your instincts and use the same tests of checking how food is cooking as you usually would. Remember too to stir, turn, rotate dishes and rearrange according to recipe or basic instructions.

★ If you are a novice microwave cook or first-time user then try the simpler recipes first before attempting more complicated recipes and wait awhile before converting your own home favourites.

★ Remember even though basic microwave only cooking, over short periods of time, will mean dishes stay cool to the touch, most combination, convection and long-cooked microwave only dishes will become hot – so oven gloves are a must.

★ When combination cooking a recipe that has no specific instructions then choose a higher temperature than normally used conventionally and a Low (30%) microwave power level. If you are not sure about the temperature then try cooking as below as a good starting point.

COMBINATION COOK at 180–200°C on LOW (30%) power

Remember to make a note of your timings and any changes you might like to make next time for better results.

★ Check that the basic descriptions used in this book relate to your model of oven before attempting to cook. If they do not then refer to the chart on page 148 for advice upon which timings and instructions to follow or what adjustments to make.

★ Like any other cooking appliance, the microwave should be treated with respect. Clean it well, service it regularly and if not under guarantee then consider a service contract or insurance.

★ NEVER use your microwave if it is damaged in any way. Never attempt to repair it yourself call in a qualified engineer.

GUIDE TO COMPARATIVE MICROWAVE OVEN CONTROL SETTINGS

Descriptions of settings used in this book (with grilling facility)	20% (Defrost)	30% (Low)		50% (Medium)		70% (Medium /High)	100% (High)
Description of settings available on popular microwave ovens	1 keep warm low 2	2 simmer 3	3 stew medium/low 4	4 defrost medium 5	5 bake medium 6	6 roast high 7–8	7 full/high normal 10

Approximate % power input	20%	30%	40%	50%	60%	70%	100%
Approximate power output in watts	160-170W	250-255W	320W	400-425W	500W	550–600W	800-850W
Cooking time in minutes (for times greater than 10 minutes simply add the figures in the appropriate columns)	4	3¼	2½	2	1¾	1¼	1
	8	6¾	5	4	3¼	2¾	2
	12	10	7½	6	5	4	3
	16	13¼	10	8	6¾	5¼	4
	20	16¾	12½	10	8¼	6¾	5
	24	20	15	12	10	8	6
	28	23½	17½	14	12	9¼	7
	32	26¾	20	16	13¼	10¾	8
	36	30	22½	18	15	12	9
	40	33¾	25	20	16½	13¼	10

Combination Microwave Convenience Food Cooking Chart

Stir, rearrange or turn over foods (where applicable) once, halfway through the cooking time. Allow a 2–5 minute standing time. Always remove from foil containers unless manufacturer's instructions indicate otherwise. Preheat the oven, if necessary, according to the manufacturer's instructions:

Item	Temperature	Microwave setting	Minutes
BAKED BEANS			
142 g (5 oz) can	–	High (100%)	1¼–2¾
220 g (7¾ oz) can	–	High (100%)	1½–2¾
447 g (15 oz) can	–	High (100%)	2½–3
BREAD, PART BAKED			
1 pkt French sticks	250°C	Medium (50%)	4–5
1 pkt hamburger rolls	250°C	Medium (50%)	1½–2½
1 pkt white rolls	250°C	Medium (50%)	4–6½
1 pkt wholewheat rolls	250°C	Medium (50%)	4–5
BREAD MIXES (made up according to packet instructions)			
900 g (2 lb) brown loaf	250°C	Medium (50%)	11–13
900 g (2 lb) white loaf	250°C	Medium (50%)	12–14
CAKE MIXES (made up according to packet instructions)			
15 cm (6 in) Madeira cake	250°C	Medium (50%)	6½–7
20 cm (8 in) round slice mix	250°C	Medium (50%)	7–8
18 cm (7 in) sponge cake (one layer to be split)	250°C	Medium (50%)	7–9
18 cm (7 in) square slice mix	250°C	Medium (50%)	8–9
CASSEROLES, READY-PREPARED			
4 portions beef casserole	–	High (100%)	7
2 portions chicken casserole	–	High (100%)	1½
6 portions chicken casserole	–	High (100%)	16
FISH IN BATTER AND CRUMBS, FROZEN			
200 g (7 oz) pkt cod steaks in batter	230°C	–	15–20
1 portion crumbled fish with 1 portion chips	250°C	Medium (50%)	7
400 g (14 oz) pkt fish in batter	250°C	Medium (50%)	11
400 g (14 oz) pkt fish in breadcrumbs	250°C	Medium (50%)	9

Item	Temperature	Microwave setting	Minutes
FISH IN SAUCE, FROZEN			
170 g (6 oz) boil in bag	–	Low (30%)	13
2 × 170 g (6 oz) boil in bags	–	Medium (50%)	11–13
FISH PIE, READY TO COOK (CHILLED)			
Family size (4 portion)	250°C	Medium (50%)	7–9
FRANKFURTERS			
425 g (15 oz) can	–	High (100%)	2–3
4 loose	–	High (100%)	3–4
450 g (1 lb) loose	–	High (100%)	7–9½
HAM, CANNED			
450 g (1 lb) joint	–	Medium (50%)	10½–13
900 g (2 lb) joint	–	Medium (50%)	21½–25
1.5 kg (3 lb) joint	–	Medium (50%)	32–38½
HOT DOG IN ROLL			
1	–	High (100%)	½–¾
LASAGNE OR MOUSSAKA, FROZEN COOKED			
Family size (4 portion)	230°C	Defrost (20%)	18–22
MEAT DISHES, CANNED			
425 g (15 oz) can mince	–	High (100%)	3¾–4
425 g (15 oz) can stew	–	High (100%)	3–3¾
1 individual steak and kidney pudding	–	High (100%)	2½–3
PASTRIES AND PIES, FROZEN READY TO BAKE (UNCOOKED)			
Apple pie, family size	230°C	Defrost (20%)	27–32
Bakewell tart, family size	230°C	Defrost (20%)	17–19
Chicken pies, 4 individual	230°C	High (100%)	18–23
Meat pie, family size	230°C	Defrost (20%)	18–23
Quiche, family size	250°C	Defrost (20%)	18–23
Sausage rolls, 12 medium	250°C	Defrost (20%)	18–23
Shepherd's pie, family size	230°C	Defrost (20%)	18–23
PASTRIES AND PIES, READY COOKED			
Apple pie, family size	250°C	Defrost (20%)	15–17
Chicken and mushroom, family size	250°C	High (100%)	9–11
Cornish pasties, 4	250°C	Defrost (20%)	11–13

Item	Temperature	Microwave setting	Minutes
PASTRIES AND PIES, READY COOKED			
Minced beef, family size	250°C	High (100%)	9–11
Quiche, family size	250°C	Defrost (20%)	11–13
Sausage rolls, 12 medium	250°C	Defrost (20%)	14–16
Shepherd's pie, family size	250°C	High (100%)	11–13
Steak and kidney, family size	250°C	High (100%)	11–13
PIZZA, FROZEN			
93 g (3¼ oz) pizza	220°C	–	10
175 g (6 oz) French bread pizza	200°C	–	15–20
PLATED MEAL, CHILLED			
1 × 350–450 g (12–16 oz)	–	High (100%)	2½–4
POTATO PRODUCTS, FROZEN			
450 g (1 lb) oven chips	250°C	Medium (50%)	13
450 g (1 lb) potato crunchies	250°C	Medium (50%)	11
450 g (1 lb) potato fritters	250°C	Medium (50%)	13
4 potato waffles	250°C	Medium (50%)	11
PUDDINGS AND DESSERTS, FROZEN READY TO BAKE			
680 g (1½ lb) apple pie	220°C	Medium (50%)	17
280 g (10 oz) apple strudel	250°C	Medium (50%)	9
10 individual apple strudels	250°C	Medium (50%)	17
450 g (1 lb) egg custard tart	220°C	Medium (50%)	17½
450 g (1 lb) fruit crumble	250°C	Medium (50%)	10
RATATOUILLE			
400 g (14 oz) can	–	High (100%)	3
RICE PUDDING			
440 g (15½ oz) can	–	High (100%)	3½–4
SAUSAGE, DELICATESSEN BOILING			
241 g (8½ oz) can	–	High (100%)	2½–3
SOUP			
283 g (10 oz) can	–	High (100%)	3–3½
SPECIAL MEALS AND DISHES, FROZEN AND READY TO COOK			
370 g (13 oz) cannelloni	250°C	Medium (50%)	12

Item	Temperature	Microwave setting	Minutes
SPECIAL MEALS AND DISHES, FROZEN AND READY TO COOK			
370 g (13 oz) pkt chicken and chips	250°C	Medium (50%)	11
340 g (12 oz) Chicken Kiev	250°C	Medium (50%)	7½
6 rissoles	250°C	Medium (50%)	5
12 rissoles	250°C	Medium (50%)	9
280 g (10 oz) veal Cordon Bleu	250°C	Medium (50%)	9
STEAMED SPONGE (removed from can)			
300 g (10½ oz) can	–	High (100%)	1½

Convection Microwave and Microwave only Convenience Food Cooking Chart

Stir, rearrange or turn over foods (where applicable) once, halfway through the cooking time. Allow a 2–5 minute standing time. Always remove from the foil containers unless convection microwave manufacturer indicates otherwise.

Preheat the convection microwave for 10 minutes, if necessary, or according to the manufacturer's instructions.

Instructions that have the symbol* refer to convection microwave ovens only.

Item	Convection Temperature	Microwave setting	Minutes
BAKED BEANS			
142 g (5 oz) can	–	High (100%)	1–1¼
220 g (7¾ oz) can	–	High (100%)	1¼–1½
447 g (15 ¾ oz) can	–	High (100%)	2–2½
CASSEROLES, READY-PREPARED			
Beef casserole, 4 portions	–	High (100%)	6½
Chicken casserole, 2 portions	–	High (100%)	1¼–1½
Chicken casserole, 6 portions	–	High (100%)	13
EGG AND BACON FLANS, FROZEN*			
4 individual flans	220°C	–	20–25
FISH IN BATTER, FROZEN*			
200 g (7 oz) cod steaks in batter	230°C	–	15–20
FISH IN SAUCE, FROZEN			
170 g (6 oz) boil in bag	–	Low (30%)	11
2 × 170 g (6 oz) boil in bags	–	Medium (50%)	9–11

Item	Convection Temperature	Microwave setting	Minutes
FRANKFURTERS			
425 g (15 oz) can	–	High (100%)	1½–2½
4 loose	–	High (100%)	2½–3½
450 g (1 lb) loose	–	High (100%)	7–9½
HAM CANNED			
450 g (1 lb) joint	–	Medium (50%)	9–11
900 g (2 lb) joint	–	Medium (50%)	18–22
1.5 kg (3 lb) joint	–	Medium (50%)	27–33
HOT DOG IN ROLL			
1	–	High (100%)	¼–½
MEAT DISHES, CANNED			
425 g (15 oz) can mince	–	High (100%)	3½
425 g (15 oz) can stew	–	High (100%)	2½–3½
1 individual steak and kidney pudding	–	High (100%)	2–2½
PIES, PASTRIES AND READY MEALS, FROZEN READY TO COOK*			
1 individual chicken and mushroom pie	220°C	–	20
184 g (6½ oz) pkt faggots in sauce	220°C	–	20–25
225 g (8 oz) shepherd's pie	220°C	–	20–25
PIZZA, FROZEN*			
175 g (6 oz) French bread pizza	200°C	–	15–20
93 g (3¼ oz) pizza	220°C	–	10
PLATED MEAL (chilled)			
1 × 350 –450 g (12–16 oz)	–	High (100%)	2–3½
POTATOES, CANNED			
283 g (10 oz) can	–	High (100%)	1½
538 g (1 lb 3 oz) can	–	High (100%)	3½
POTATO PRODUCTS, FROZEN (cook in a preheated browning dish)			
175 g (6 oz) oven chips	–	High (100%)	5–6½
350 g (12 oz) oven chips	–	High (100%)	10–11
4 potato croquettes	–	High (100%)	3½–4
8 potato croquettes	–	High (100%)	6½–7
16 potato croquettes	–	High (100%)	13–14
100 g (4 oz) potato shapes	–	High (100%)	3½–4
225 g (8 oz) potato shapes	–	High (100%)	4–6

Item	Convection Temperature	Microwave setting	Minutes
POTATO PRODUCTS, FROZEN (cook in a preheated browning dish)			
450 g (1 lb) potato shapes	–	High (100%)	8–10
4 potato waffles	–	High (100%)	5–6½
RATATOUILLE			
400 g (14 oz) can	–	High (100%)	2½
RICE PUDDING			
440 g (15½ oz) can	–	High (100%)	3–4
SAUSAGE, DELICATESSEN BOILING			
214 g (8½ oz) pkt	–	High (100%)	1½–2½
SOUP			
283 g (10 oz) can	–	High (100%)	2½–3
STEAMED SPONGE (removed from can)			
300 g (10½ oz) can	–	High (100%)	1¼–1¾

INDEX